RAISING CHILDREN
FOR
SUCCESS

RAISING CHILDREN
FOR
SUCCESS

Blueprints
and
Building Blocks
For
Developing
Capable People

by H. STEPHEN GLENN

with JANE NELSEN

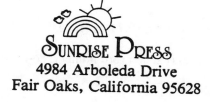

SUNRISE PRESS
4984 Arboleda Drive
Fair Oaks, California 95628

Raising Children For Success: Blueprints And Building Blocks For Developing Capable People

Cover Design by Susan Hull

Printed in the United States of America

Library of Congress catalog card number: 86-62001

ISBN: 0-9606896-4-8

"In times of change, learners inherit the earth, while the learned find themselves beautifully equipped to deal with a world that no longer exists."

Eric Hoffer

This Book is Dedicated

To Learners Everywhere

ACKNOWLEDGEMENTS

We would like to acknowledge that our understanding of this topic has been greatly heightened and enhanced by thousands of people over the last twenty years who have shared with us their personal struggles and their personal successes in the hope that they would increase people's understanding of families in our changing world.

I, Stephen Glenn, would like to acknowledge Tricia's role as my partner and friend in marriage for twenty years and mother of our four biological children and many others who have needed her over the years. She provides the inspiration and follow-through in doing such a great job with our young people in a way that leaves me free to talk confidently about their successful development.

I would like to acknowledge our four children, Keri Marie, Kristi Lyn, Kimbi Lee, and Michael who have raised a fairly capable father and have been willing to help me go through the trial and error process in learning to be one.

I would also like to acknowledge Jane who challenged me to sit down and record the many thoughts and ideas spoken in my workshops and speeches over the years. Without her discipline this book might never have been written.

I, Jane Nelsen, would like to acknowledge the inspiration Steve has been in my life as in so many others. The principles presented in this book have been extremely helpful in our family. It is a privilege to be instrumental in making this material available in book form.

Special appreciation goes to Barry, Mark, and Mary for their patience, support, and self-reliance during this project and in general. They are extremely capable people.

CONTENTS

Introduction 11

1. Families in Transition 21

2. Lost in the Shuffle 33

3. Perception 47

4. Developing Strong Perceptions of
   Personal Capabilities 63

5. Helping Children Feel Meaning,
   Purpose, and Significance 87

6. Helping Children Develop a Perception of
   Having Control Over Their Environment 105

7. Helping Children Develop Strong
   Intra-personal Skills 121

8. Helping Children Develop Strong
   Interpersonal Skills 135

9. Helping Children Develop Strong
   Systemic Skills 149

10. Helping Children Develop Strong
    Judgmental Skills 165

11. Blueprints For Success 177

12. The Price of Change 191

Bibliography 207

INTRODUCTION

Americans, like people of many other nations, are crossing a frontier of knowledge and technology expanding at a rate unprecedented in history. Nowhere is the stress of that journey more evident than among American families and young people.

DECLINING ACHIEVEMENT, MOTIVATION, AND DISCIPLINE

The steadily emerging base of statistical evidence in the United States indicates that beginning with the children born in 1946, who became the class of '63, achievement began a steady downward trend that persisted over the next twenty years. That wonderful, flock of postwar children, born so hopefully in 1946, struggled to reach their potential. They took the achievement tests in 1963 and became the first group of children in 100 years to move significantly *downward* instead of *upward* in their scores. They also set records in the problem areas for teenagers today: crime and vandalism, teenage pregnancy, drug and alcohol abuse, and teenage suicide.

Their record stood only one year as each group of children, without exception from 1963 to 1983, followed their lead and dropped lower in achievement scores, motivation, and discipline while increased numbers participated in the problem areas for teenagers.

In retrospect, the group of young people to turn downward in achievement were the front ranks of the *baby boom*. Being born in 1946, they inherited an entire new lifestyle, changing rapidly from rural/small town settings to an urban/suburban environment which included new inventions from radio through television, to supersonic space travel and lasers.

The enormous changes that have occurred since the *baby boom* began created conditions from which we have inherited remarkable opportunities but have also inherited liabilities. These liabilities are mainly in the form of changes in lifestyle which left our culture weaker in support systems for people. Later we will discuss how we can compensate for these loses and eliminate these liabilities.

CHANGES SINCE THE BABY BOOM BEGAN

For centuries, generations of people were raised in the lifestyle and traditions of their parents. In that process they adapted to the traditions and developed the basic capabilities to function effectively within this lifestyle and to maintain relatively stable families.

At the end of World War II, thousands of families moved away from networks of grandmothers, grandfathers, aunts, uncles, cousins, nieces, and nephews into new communities. They left small towns, villages, and farms that were the basis for family life and found themselves in larger urban and suburban settings. By 1986 the average family was moving every 2-1/2 years and knew very little about their neighbors and relatives.

The smaller, more stable population settings had offered opportunities for children to learn life skills through on-the-job training because they were needed to help the family function and survive. In the new urban/suburban settings, children are not needed in the day to day functioning of families and frequently spend a large portion of their time watching television, which includes a variety of programs and concepts that are counter-productive to the development of skills and capabilities necessary for successful living.

Increasing numbers of children had fewer and fewer opportunities to experience a meaningful role in family life and in the traditions of the culture. *Without a meaningful role it was difficult to develop a sense of meaning, purpose, and significance to their lives through being needed, listened to, and taken seriously.*

The struggle to raise capable children became more difficult for families who had not learned to compensate for the things that were lost in the rapid lifestyle changes. Capabilities which had been acquired so naturally in the old circumstances, began to weaken. The lack of strength in skills and capabilities threatened the potential of young people.

STRESSFUL RELATIONSHIPS

During that same period, relationships between spouses became more tenuous and stressful. Many families experienced a rapid increase in reported incidents of spouse abuse, child abuse, desertion, neglect, and sedative and alcohol dependency. In part this was reflected by increased statistical awareness. However, whenever appropriate controls were applied there also appears to have been a significant increase in the incidence of these problems.

Overall, we can say that stability within relationships for

couples, relationships between parents and children, and the interaction between families, individuals, and the systems around them, such as jobs, schools, and communities, became more turbulent than they appear to have been in the decades before.

GREAT AMERICAN DREAM FALTERING

As America passed through the 60's, it became almost a platitude to suggest that the great American dream was faltering. We confused ourselves in many ways in our attempt to explain what was happening to us. Since the 60's were turbulent, we looked for answers within the 60's. We tried desperately to find the cause.

Some theorists suggested we were the terminal victims of urbanization, technology, future shock, and the bomb threat. Conservatives suggested that we were the victims of divorce, working mothers, and single parent families, and that as long as we faced these conditions, we had to accept our struggle as normal.

Some *dropouts* of the 60's were happy to support these theories. If it was suggested to them that perhaps the reason they did not want to apply themselves was due to the bomb threat, they would readily agree. They would not admit that they simply preferred to sit around and get *high* rather than use self-discipline and hard work to apply themselves.

Once we came to our senses and began to look more thoughtfully at the situation, it became clear that we could not blame any single factor for producing the conditions we were dealing with. Different accumulations of several factors were contributing to stress and vulnerability in a variety of patterns for family systems.

HOPEFUL OUTLOOK

To suggest that one factor was responsible was much like saying one snowflake caused an avalanche or that one grain of sand tipped the balance on a scale. So we began to look for *factors* that could *contribute*, took a longer view, and saw the 60's as a product of the 30's, 40's, and 50's.

We also began to look more carefully at individuals who were *not* having such negative experiences and who were doing well in spite of urbanization, technology, single parent status, divorce, poverty, affluence, and future shock. This produced a more hopeful perspective.

From a developmental point of view, when we go back to 1946, the year children from the High School Class of '63 were born, and explore the changes that occurred between their birth and their emergence into young adulthood, we find many factors that had the power to shift, alter and weaken the dimensions of family life and culture.

It is now apparent that the problem was not necessarily technology and urbanization but our lack of understanding about how to compensate for the changes these processes brought about. We need to take a look at our understanding, our priorities, and our processes for living in our world. This is a far more hopeful outlook. With this change in perspective we are discovering a wealth of options.

BREAKTHROUGH

As we look more closely and do a more thoughtful comparison of uniquely successful individuals and families who live alongside individuals who are average or below average in their struggles and productivity, we begin to achieve many breakthroughs in our understanding. We are finding models that all of us can use. Studying the lives of unusually successful families and individuals in today's world points the way toward a more successful future.

Research today gives us a primary hold on many of the factors that contributed to the upward trend in problem areas. We know that many of the problems facing young people appear to stem from the same, or a very similar, set of factors. The factors that predict or produce one of these problems tend to be the same or similar factors that predict or produce the others.

We can avoid replicating the downward trends in achievement and self-discipline and the upward trends in crime and vandalism, teenage pregnancy, drug and alcohol abuse, and teenage suicide. In future chapters we will deal with the factors which contribute to these problems and show how to take out insurance against the problem areas for young people.

SLOW ACCEPTANCE OF NEW KNOWLEDGE

The field of family and human relations is benefiting from the incredible explosion of knowledge and technology. This information is very exciting. However, new knowledge is usually accepted very slowly.

There was a time when one out of every four times a woman gave birth to a baby, she or the baby died in the process or soon after from a disease called *childbirth fever.* We now know the deaths were caused by infections from bacteria introduced by the physician's unclean hands.

The physician who discovered that by washing his hands he could reduce the mortality rate to only 8% was considered a quack by his colleagues and died in professional disrepute. It took more than 100 years, and the work of Pasteur with bacteria, before the medical community was convinced and doctors began washing their hands.

Hopefully it will not take 100 years for the new knowledge we have about families to be accepted and used effectively. The evidence is strong that our hopes are not misplaced.

FATHERS JOINING THE TEAM

We, the authors, have been doing programs on *Raising Capable Young People* for many years. Several years ago 90% of our participants were female, and it was very clear the culture still believed that raising children was *woman's work*. It has been very pleasing the last few years to see that over one-third of our participants, daytime or nighttime, are fathers who have declared their interest and decided parenting is a collaborative project in which all need to be involved.

A few years ago, in a little town outside of Indianapolis, we were doing a community awareness series. As part of that series we held an evening on *Fathering for Fathers*. Ten fathers showed up — nine of them married to the committee members who planned it and one who got stuck in his driveway without an alibi and was dragged to the occasion. By contrast, we held another series in that same community recently, and 390 fathers came and gave us a standing-room only crowd. They came in spite of the fact that the school, long after this event had been scheduled and advertised, had decided to hold a Sports Appreciation Banquet at the same time.

To their credit, over 200 fathers organized, went to the banquet, paid for their spaghetti, shook hands with the coaches and then announced, "The best thing we can do to support this program is to get our act together as fathers. Any of you that agree, come with us." One hundred and ninety of those fathers left the banquet and came to the session on fathering. We feel this interest represents an increasingly hopeful and persistent trend.

BABY BOOMERS AS FATHERS

There was much speculation on what *baby boomers* would be like as parents after going through so much turmoil and turbulence. A recent Time/Life Survey indicated that *baby boomers,* as fathers, are spending four to five times the amount of personal time educating two children than their fathers spent devoted to five children.

This could explain why a significant number of young people are now becoming more achievement orientated and have greater admiration for their parents. Two thirds of all American young people recently surveyed indicated that they had substantial admiration for their parents and considered them among their heroes. We believe this increased interest among fathers to be actively involved in the process of raising children will help offset the pressures placed on mothers by the changing economic conditions that have removed many of them from the home for significant periods of time.

UPWARD TREND BEGINNING

Each year we watch the National Senior Survey, which is a detailed study of the attitudes of high school graduates. In 1978 and 1979, this survey indicated an all time low percentage of young people who had a strong future orientation, clear goals, or assertiveness about personal beliefs. The survey showed that those characteristics had declined coincidentally with the increase in marijuana use among young people.

In more recent National Senior Surveys, 1983 through 1985, a reversal of these trends was observed. They found significantly more involvement with things like student government, community service, goal orientation toward the future and coincidentally, a decline in the use of marijuana among young people. These classes also did better on the achievement tests than previous classes from previous years. One sobering note is the realization that in the 1986 National Senior Survey some of these upward trends appeared to be stagnating, at least temporarily. We cannot rest on slight gains.

LIMITED ONLY BY OUR ABILITY TO DREAM

It has been said very well that *a nation that does not stand firmly for something will ultimately stand for anything.* The turbulence of the 60's and 70's presented a number of problems for our communities and our families which caused us to became so busy trying to prevent things from going wrong that we appeared to lose sight of what we were trying to accomplish.

It is more productive to develop a vision of who we are, where we can go, and what we can accomplish. When this is shared with our children, both as a belief and as a set of experiences, it may inspire them to work toward these ends. The *Great American Dream* does not need to die. Right now it is like a garden suffering from lack of cultivation.

NEED FOR LEARNERS

Perhaps our challenge in the face of so much change, particularly the challenge for all of us who raise and educate young people, is stated best by Eric Hoffer:

"In times of change, learners inherit the earth, while the learned find themselves beautifully equipped to deal with a world that no longer exists."

A theologian recently pointed out that a similar injunction was offered by Christ in the New Testament when he said, "Blessed are the meek, for they shall inherit the earth." The meek in that context did not mean weak, down-looking individuals, but those humble enough to be teachable.

In whatever form we find it, this counsel is important for us today. We face challenges unprecedented in history. We cannot be arrogant enough to say, "Well, that is the way my parents did it," or "Our family always handled it that way." We must look thoughtfully and ask, "What was it we were accomplishing in our family by doing it that way?" and "What ways do we have today to accomplish that same thing?"

Splitting the wood and walking to the cowshed gave us the physical activity necessary for our bodies to maintain health as well as to get needed chores done. Today we may need to compensate and participate in recreational walking, aerobics, or a workout center to accomplish the same benefits.

In this same sense, we can compensate for the continuing rapid changes of our society by thoughtfully learning how to prepare our young people to have the tools, the capabilities, and the beliefs of the learner.

EDUCATION FOR FAMILY LIVING

Society gives a great deal of approval to anyone who pursues an education for career training or professional development but has not yet acknowledged a need for this same kind of vigorous exploration in the area of family and personal relationships.

The pioneers who explored and settled our continent found

that they had to be very assertive in assembling around campfires to talk with scouts and fellow travelers to explore the wisdom they were gaining from the journey. Like them we can ask friends and neighbors for information, read books, attend classes, and talk openly about the struggles and dilemmas we face and be thoughtful about this process. We can then use our own wisdom to apply any knowledge we gain in ways that are adapted to our unique life situation.

MUST BE LEARNERS RATHER THAN LEARNED

Human knowledge in our culture is expanding at the rate of 100% every five years. In some fields a 100% gain in new knowledge every eleven months is not unusual. Many futurists project that, if these trends continue, the first graders this year must be equipped on graduation day to handle a 100% explosion of knowledge every 38 days. If we think about that, it means the information in every book they read the first of the month needs to be upgraded by the end of the month. In this kind of a world we have to be certain that we give them the generic tools of the learner, rather than the accumulated data of the past which the learned once carried into the future. It is a great challenge.

TOOLS OF THE LEARNER

In studying the characteristics of learners, we have identified a number of critical capabilities and beliefs which will be referred to in later chapters as the *significant seven*.

Among the *significant seven* are three beliefs or perceptions of the world and four skills which consistently carry people across the gulf of the unknown and allow them to unlock much of their potential. However, to help young people adequately develop these perceptions and skills will require changes in the practices of many parents and teachers. It will also require a significant alteration of the experience base of many young people to allow them opportunities to develop the necessary perceptions and skills for successful living.

We are beginning to recognize that many of our problems are largely due to default rather than to design. We can design training programs for our children at home and school that will bring more consistently positive responses.

HABILITATION

The process of growing from weak to strong, from dependent to independent, from incapable to capable is called habilitation.

I spent eight years in higher education studying rehabilitation and never once discussed habilitation. It was my young daughter who really challenged me one day. She was learning about dictionaries and wanted to help me with a paper I was working on, so I asked her to look up *rehabilitation.*

The definition she found was: *to rehabilitate means to restore to former excellence.*

I began to laugh. My daughter asked, "Dad, why are you laughing?"

I replied, "I was just thinking about all my clients. It is hard for me to believe that every struggling adolescent was once an excellent individual who forgot how. It is hard for me to believe that every struggling alcoholic was once an excellent recovering alcoholic and gave it up for some unknown reason. I can't believe that every chronically inadequate family was once an excellent family and lost sight of it. It is my impression that virtually all of the people I have served in my career have been struggling to attain something for the first time that had never been within reach for them."

She said, "Well, Dad, didn't you always tell me that when you look up a word with "re" in front of it that it is very helpful to look up the word without the "re" in front of it to see what it is you are redoing?"

I said, "Yes, that does make sense."

"Well then," she said, "we should look up *habilitation.*"

We could not find the word habilitation in our Webster's Dictionary. She pointed out that there was a bigger dictionary at the library. So we went to the library and searched through that big, moldy dictionary, and she said with excitement, "It's here!"

The definition given was: *to habilitate means to clothe.* That didn't ring a bell, so we looked up the reference that was given which led us to a chart showing the evolution of the human race. On the chart there was a series of figures beginning with hairy apes that stood increasingly upright until they ended up in a three piece suit with a brief case. These figures were all naked and hairy until the middle of the chart when one of them put on fur jogging shorts. The first one to go from naked to clothed was called homo habilus — man the able or capable.

From the root word habilus we get ability or capability. The first alleged progenitor of the human race who acquired capabilities to act on the environment rather than react to it was called *human the able or capable*. It was the capabilities that distinguished humans from animals.

When we found the definition, she said with marvelous childlike logic, "Then aren't you trying to do something that was never done in the first place?"

I said, "Where were you about 30 billion dollars worth of federal programs ago with that kind of logic and insight?"

For years many organizations and institutions have tried to rehabilitate people who have never been habilitated in the first place, since rehabilitation means to restore to former excellence.

Human beings arrive in this world without capabilities and have to acquire them in an apprenticeship. All the things that have happened during the massive changes our culture has gone through have undercut the family's ability to provide opportunities for young people to engage in an apprenticeship of habilitation to prepare them for life.

Most people in rehabilitation programs have never been capable, productive or independent. In reality they do not need rehabilitation. They need habilitation.

OUR FOCUS

In the following chapters we focus on the *significant seven* as building blocks for developing (habilitating) capable young people and will blueprint the strategies and the activities through which parents, teachers, and other significant adults can encourage young people to develop beneficial perceptions, skills, and capabilities. We analyze the research on success and outline the kinds of beliefs and understandings of life that appear to best prepare people to act confidently and to take the initiative in whatever aspects of life they wish to pursue.

It is our sincere hope that through this process we can give encouragement and direction to the efforts of parents, teachers, families and most importantly, young people, to make their potential more accessible to them.

Chapter 1

FAMILIES IN TRANSITION

In 1930 Steve and Jane were enthusiastic about finding ways to improve their lot in life. They had to work hard to help their families make it through the depression and war. If they got their chores done, they would have time to include school in their daily activities. They were respectful and obedient to their elders. Their achievement test scores reflected the many capabilites they had developed of self-discipline, responsibility, judgement, and perseverance.

In 1980 their grandchildren, Billy and Jeanne, thought school was *a bore*. They were more interested in avoiding hard work and effort than in trying to improve their lot in life. They had never had to work for anything. Why start now? They wanted excitement in life and turned to television, drugs, alcohol, and sex to find immediate gratification. They were often sullen and disrespectful to their elders. Their achievement test scores reflected their underdeveloped motivation and capabilities.

THE GOOD OLD DAYS

What happened during those forty years? Why is it that during a time of relative prosperity, when children have more opportunities and possibilities for achievement and success than ever before, they seem less success oriented and capable than ever before? What was it about the *good old days* that helped children develop more capabilities than they have today?

The *good old days* were not so good, they are just old. However, many things were happening then that helped children develop the capabilities that are necessary for success.

THESE ARE THE BEST OF TIMES

The world we are in now is a much better world by many standards. The world is, however, very different than it was 40 years ago. Forty years ago and more, we could assume that children growing up, if they survived physically, would emerge having developed the basic capabilities needed to respond to life and any opportunities that might exist. They were usually equipped to act and make choices even though there were not many options available.

For centuries parents worried about how they could find opportunities for themselves and for their children to have more than they did. Many of our ancestors, motivated by the possibility of greater opportunities in America, decided they would sleep in the bottoms of ships and risk a 35% mortality rate, knowing that one third of the people on the ship would die before the ship reached the other shore. They hoped to be lucky enough to survive, and to find room to own a piece of land, unlike their families who had only been tenants for centuries. Some risked their lives for the dream of owning a business and the possibility even to get rich so their children could do better than they did.

They came to America, faced an alien environment, and claimed the largest country with the most riches in the shortest time in history. They did this with self-confidence, courage, and assertiveness, not by sitting around watching the world vicariously on television.

Their children usually continued working hard to improve the land or business their parents had worked and died for. In so doing, they continued to develop capabilities. Many of these children were all dressed up in capabilities, with limited opportunities.

Today we children stand semi-naked in capabilities, in front of incredible possibilities. Our challenge today is to help our children develop self-reliance, commitment, and the skills and capabilities children learned 30 to 50 years ago because they were genuinely needed by their family in the economic life of the family and because they grew up in stable cultures with roles and traditions for them to follow.

To some extent the assumptions that young people would follow the same roles as their parents were oppressive. Nevertheless, by going through those motions, children served an apprenticeship in most of the basic realities that would confront them as adults stepping out into life. By the time they reached adolescence, there were very few mysteries about what a crop failure meant, about what it took to get from place to place, about how long the family had to save to buy new shoes or some special thing for Christmas.

There were also many mysteries for adolescents. What was romance all about? What happened once you got married? Children had no real awareness of what adults talked about when they were together. The child culture consisted of siblings and cousins, interacting with older and younger siblings, rather than peer groups of the same age.

That environment had a number of assets in the area of an internship for life. There were many resources to encourage self-discipline, judgement, and responsibility. On the down side, it had a lot of limitations. In the good old days people did not have the benefits of technology. Travel took a long time. It was difficult to communicate with people who lived far away. There were very few jobs and opportunities. Most young people could only hope to follow in their parents' footsteps, work the family farm, grow up in the family business, or, if the family was poor and destitute, struggle for survival and the possibility of doing a slight bit better.

The hope of getting an education was a rare thing for many because they started working very early in their life and couldn't get the time free. The hope to be able to write and read and maybe become a learned person was a fantasy for most people.

They were largely clothed in most capabilities for the journey of life. They were equipped not only to survive but to advance their condition. However, many were frustrated by the limitations of the opportunities to fulfill their capabilities.

Then, in almost a quantum leap at the end of World War II, we were thrust in two decades onto a totally new frontier, where opportunities were exploding, travel was easy, communication was efficient, and opportunities were expanding. However, the cost of all these opportunities has been a dislocation in most of our basic training mechanisms for young people.

STARVATION IN THE FACE OF A BANQUET

Today we are finding that across the nation as a whole, far too many Americans find themselves at the onset of puberty facing an incredible smorgasbord of challenges and opportunities but are frequently deficient in many of the capabilities, including self-confidence, validation, self-discipline, judgement, and responsibility, to constructively carve out assets for themselves.

Today most children will be forced to accept more years of education than most people in history ever fantasized they would have an opportunity for in a lifetime. Education sometimes seems like a curse for many young people today.

Young people who had to split cords of firewood, chase animals that got through the neighbor's fence, walk behind the mule for hours plowing, cook large meals for farm laborers, or hike two miles into town and back to get the mail or supplies, sometimes viewed school as a wonderful alternative. Parents could say, "Listen, if you don't want to be in school, that's okay. You can just come and join us in our work." Compared with school, that was a very heavy challenge. Today when children are not in school, they have snack foods, frisbees, rock videos, soap operas, wandering around town, smoking a little dope, drinking a few six-pacs. Compared to that, school is not so attractive for many.

We live in the best of all times, but we have a different challenge. The explosion of change has brought us to the point where we can now assume the opportunities only dreamed of by previous generations. We now have to stop and lay a foundation of capabilities and preparation that those generations could take for granted.

We have, in short, the best challenge. It is far better to be standing semi-naked in front of fantastic possibilities than to be clothed for a journey and then frustrated by the lack of opportunity.

VALUES PASSED ON

There was a time in America when the attitudes, values, and behavior of each generation were effectively passed on to the next generation through interaction between the generations. Teenage boys and girls could step in and fill the roles of their mothers and fathers if they needed to because of death or illness because they had been actively associated with these roles from infancy.

The lifestyle was essentially rural/small town. Children often worked ten hours a day alongside one or both parents. Children received on-the-job training as they watched their parents doing essential, practical things, making decisions, and discussing values. Very early children became participants, rather than just observers, in the work-a-day adult world.

During the remaining few hours, after the work was done, children participated in mealtime discussions, learning handicrafts, making clothing or items actually used in the home or for work. There was a great deal of interaction between brothers and sisters, parents and children, grandparents and other relatives as they worked together, played together, and often learned to read and write from each other.

SUPPORT FROM FAMILY NETWORKS

There were many benefits of having this network of extended family. If Dad came down on his son very heavily, Grandma was there to say, "He was like that when he was a boy, too; but you had better go along and do what he says."

In this way, even the heaviest authoritarian discipline was rationalized and personalized for the child so that he could understand and accept it more easily. If a father was too harsh with a child, Grandma could soften the effect by explaining, "Your father forgets that he was the same way as a boy, but you had better do what he says." Authoritarian discipline was workable because other adults were around to offer explanations and affirmations.

LEARNING FROM CONSEQUENCES

Even small children had chores that were important personal responsibilities. If the child assigned to do the milking forgot to milk the cow for three days, the family went without milk until the cow had another calf. Weeding was not busy work. If the children did not pull the weeds, in three months there would be no vegetables to eat. The three-year-old child knew how important it was to gather eggs every day so his family could have eggs for breakfast.

Most children grew up with capabilities because much of their experience involved significance, meaning, purpose, and relevance. They were often needed, respected, and taken seriously.

The rural population had very limited access to information. Parents formed groups, pooled resources, and hired a teacher whose values and behavior were in harmony with their own.

The home and school, in partnership, had the job of preparing individuals for successful living. It was a lifestyle in which raising capable young people was a natural result of constant on-the-job training for adulthood.

RAPID CHANGE

Between 1935 and 1950, the greatest social change ever known in this country took place in an amazing fifteen years time. In 1930, according to the census, seventy percent of all Americans lived on farms or in small communities. By 1950 there had been a complete reversal. Nearly seventy percent lived in an urban/suburban environment, and only one third on farms or in small communities. By 1970, there was an increase to nearly eighty percent of all Americans living in an urban/suburban setting. Even those living in a rural environment lived an urban lifestyle. They commuted to work, had television, and bused children to school. In just thirty-five years American made a transition which had taken nearly 400 years in Europe without *anyone* moving *anywhere*.

WAGONS TO AUTOS

The integrity of relationships diminished all the way around when families moved from living rooms filled with dialogue as a center of family experience to family rooms dominated by television sets that preempted dialogue.

We once had kitchens filled with rituals, traditions, and collaboration where dialogue at the supper table, extending until bedtime, was frequently the most affirming and attractive of activities available. This was replaced with a room full of technology, where we fill one machine with noise, turn on another machine to watch, and wipe out all personal interaction.

We moved from wagons, which moved so slowly that we had no alternative but to talk with each other, to metal cylinders moving quickly down freeways with cassette tape players, graphic equalizers, and FM radios that made it possible to go all the way across the country and never have to say more than, "Are you sure you have to go now?"

THE END OF THE EXTENDED FAMILY

In 1940 approximately 60 to 70% of all households in America had at least one grandparent as a full time active member of the household. Today less than 2% have a grandparent available as a resource. In 1940 over 90% of all households had a full time homemaker spending approximately 39 hours a week on domestic chores.

HOME FROM WORK AND TIRED

Today close to 88% of all children who return home from school in America will enter a household where every living member has been gone the best ten hours of that day and is now coming home where all the routine business of the household must still be done. Today it takes an average of 37 hours a week to accomplish the domestic chores, but in most households there is no one around all day to do these chores. The need to get chores done after a long day at work competes with any remaining time for quality family interaction.

By the time we scurry around getting food on the table, washing and sorting clothes, taking care of other chores, issuing warnings, maybe a moment in the tub, that is it for the day. If we are not careful, we sacrifice the one thing we can't afford to lose — the dialogue and collaboration which affirms us.

LOSS OF TRADITIONS AND NETWORKS

Large communities are not the problem. The European migrants who moved to large cities in the United States prior to World War II stayed together in small districts with relatives and friends where they continued to live much the same as they had in their old country. These people went to the same church, had the same festivals, maintained the old traditions, and put their children in neighborhood schools which were frequently taught by people of the same ethnic background.

The Asian community in San Francisco had an exemplary record in terms of stability and lack of involvement with the criminal justice and social welfare systems until the end of World War II when they began to move away from their support systems and became part of the amorphous, urban/suburban lifestyle.

Urbanization was not the problem. The way we did it was the problem. We left behind rituals, traditions, culture, networks, and support systems and became isolated.

In 1930, children spent three to four hours per day personally involved with various members of the extended family - - parents, grandparents, aunts, uncles, and cousins who lived close by. Today's typical youngster has a very different experience. The extended family has been reduced to what we now call the nuclear family — one or two parents plus the children. Relatives typically live far away.

Interaction within nuclear families today has been reduced to only a few minutes per day. Of these few minutes, over half are used in one-way, negatively toned communications of parents issuing warnings or reproaching children for things done wrong.

Consider the impact of this rapid social transition on the amount and quality of family interaction alone. Urbanization has virtually eliminated the likelihood that a child would work for any significant portion of this time alongside either of his parents.

TELEVISION WAS BORN

In the 1940's, a technological innovation was introduced that was destined to have a massive social impact: television. Television, with all its good effects, has also introduced into the average home, attitudes, values, and behaviors completely foreign to most parents. Television has a tremendous influence in the home.

Of greater significance is the fact that television has become the hub of social and leisure time in our society. In 1970, the average American watched television for five hours per day.

If work time, travel time to and from work, sleep time, and viewing time average 23 hours of the day in a family, there is just one hour in twenty-four left for family interaction. This leaves out mealtimes and the normal business of the family. But Americans are ingenious! They discovered mealtime and viewing time could be combined. Of course, this is done at the expense of all the discussion and sharing that used to take place at the dinner table. If a family diligently uses 45 minutes of the remaining hour every day for routine duties, that leaves fifteen minutes per day of meaningful interaction time.

In less than thirty years we have gone from a society with a surplus of significant interactions between the generations, particularly within the primary family unit, to a society in which there is a critical shortage of that kind of significant interaction.

At the very time this has happened to families, there has also been a major change occurring in schools.

A CRISES FOR HOSPITALS AND SCHOOLS

An enormous number of new couples, who married after the war, enthusiastically sought opportunities in urban communities. They had come from rural/small town settings where there was room and resources to handle five or more children in a family. Without even checking to see if that would work in their new urban/suburban environment, they set out to continue the tradition of having five or more children. They assumed the new opportunities would make it better for children and that they would get rich and be able to provide for them. And so, a crisis began subtly in 1946. The crisis showed up first at hospitals.

In 1946 the number of births more than doubled in the urban/suburban setting that was not equipped to handle the results of this rapid change in fertility. A record number of children arrived suddenly in one year. Hospitals were overtaxed, and a significant number of children born in 1946 arrived in hallways, waiting rooms, or wherever makeshift facilities could be provided.

No one heeded this warning. These children lived five years before it occurred to anyone that they would soon be going to school.

On or around September 1, 1951, a mass of 4.2 million urban/suburban babies hit the schools looking for classrooms, teachers and books. Suddenly, without warning, 25 times the number of children who had arrived the year before to start the first grade arrived at school and said, "Where is my seat?"

School people asked, "Where did you come from?"

Kids said, "We've been here five years. We thought you saw us coming."

We hadn't. In an hour's time they forced a total change in the system. Overnight we threw together what was later called "a maladaptive response to a crisis situation," and called it public education. In the subsequent 30 years, data suggests that it has not worked for many, and has been toxic to quite a few students and teachers.

Besides the increase in dropping out and resistance from those who now had the *opportunity* to go to school, we found that the tenure of teachers hired into this new system decreased steadily. By the early 1980's, 13 years was considered to be the normal tenure after which the average teacher would discontinue his or her profession in spite of seven years of preparation.

When asked why they were quitting, the most common response was, "Everywhere I go in my profession there are too many in the same place at the same time with too much to do and too little time to do it. And I'm getting depressed watching young people slip away for lack of a few minutes of attention and encouragement that I never seem to be able to get around to giving to them. I'm hoping that by changing careers now, perhaps to social work, real estate, or counseling somewhere, I can contribute to someone's life before my career is over."

REDUCED AIR-TIME FOR DIALOGUE

At the same time we found that young people who needed more dialogue and collaboration — gifted children, those who functioned better in listening and speaking than they did in reading and writing, children with differences in how they learn (whether we call them learning disabled or just significantly unique human beings) — began to fade away in a system overcrowded with stereotypical assumptions such as delivering curriculum on the assumption that all ten-year-olds would be ready for the same thing on the same day and could be tested and evaluated based on their responses.

In the one-room schoolhouse the older kids acted as teachers' aides and tutors for the younger kids. Tutoring gave the older ones a meaningful role and the younger ones someone to work with them individually.

When the baby boom hit the urban/suburban schools, we grouped students by chronological age and sent all the tutors and teacher's aides away to their own classrooms. Then we put as many as 40 or more children in a single classroom with only one teacher without teachers' aides. The air-time for dialogue declined dramatically with 30 to 40 kids for fifty minutes, minus 20 minutes for required housekeeping activities. That left only about 40 seconds for any child to speak his or her mind each hour if each child got his or her share. However, if the teacher decided to take a few minutes, or another child got excited and spoke for a couple of minutes instead of only 40 seconds, several other children had to forfeit their time for that hour.

We shifted to a teacher dependent model in which the teacher prepared and presented the lessons, lectured, instructed, explained, and moralized. Children were taught to passively return back what the teacher had given them.

In one-room schools the teacher gave students assignments at their level and later checked out their mastery. Students were at all different levels chronologically and developmentally and thus received the work they were ready for, rather than the work the teacher was ready to present.

Since dialogue and collaboration have diminished at school, it is important that they be increased at home to produce growth and learning for young people. But we have already looked at the changes in homes. The lack of dialogue and collaboration in both homes and schools has produced double digit deflation in these most important factors.

The importance of dialogue and collaboration is now surfacing consistently in the research as the foundations of moral and ethical development, critical thinking, judgmental maturity, and effectiveness in teaching. A lack of dialogue and collaboration between the more mature and less mature decreases bonds of closeness, trust, dignity, and respect.

This lack of dialogue and collaboration in our homes and schools created a serious crises for our culture. When adults lecture, instruct, explain, or moralize to young people as their primary teaching method, young people run to their peer group as their primary basis for learning and developing an identity. When peers have dialogue with peers, all they achieve is naive clarity. *Peer* means the same level of insight, awareness, and maturity. So, how can any group of young people become aware of things that none of them are aware they need to be aware of?

It is only when the *more mature*, either in the form of teachers, siblings, or parents, collaborate with and work together with young people in learning situations and then through dialogue encourage them to develop and clarify their thinking, do young people move upward in all the areas of judgmental maturity.

By the early 1960's we were observing young people who were less mature and more vulnerable in the areas of moral and ethical development, critical thinking, and judgmental maturity. They had very weak bonds of closeness and trust in their relationships with parents and teachers and were far more tightly welded to the peer group than previous generations.

THE OVERALL IMPACT

The chart on the following page summarizes the changes which have significantly affected the family and the development of capabilities in young people by drastically reducing dialogue and collaboration and the bonds of closeness and trust that can only be built within families through a base of shared experience.

The changes which the family has undergone have been so dramatic and so rapid that family patterns have been unable to accommodate them; hence, traditional child rearing processes no longer adequately meet the needs of a majority of young people.

Significant adults can plan the kinds of activities that will help children become successful, capable people. This is not done by going back to the old ways but by understanding the principles by which human beings become capable and being sure those principles are addressed today.

The following chapters show us how to compensate for what has been lost in the transition and ensure that children develop skills and capabilities which lead to successful living.

MAJOR TRANSITIONS IN LIFESTYLE

CHARACTERISTICS	NORM 1930	NORM 1980
Family interaction	high	low
Value system	homogeneous	heterogeneous
Role models	consonant	dissonant
Logical consequences	experienced	avoided
Inter-generational associations	many	few
Education	less	more
Level of information	low	high
Technology	low	high
Non-negotiable tasks	many	few
Family work	much	little
Family size	large	small
Family dominant	extended	nuclear
Step/Blended/Single Parent Families	few (10-15%)	many (35-42%)
Class Size (K-12)	18-22	28-35
Neighborhood Schools	dominant	rare

Chapter 2

LOST IN THE SHUFFLE

As a culture we tend to devalue that which is commonplace and readily available and often look back nostalgically upon the past, which we have not experienced, and call it the *good old days*.

When we are more objective, we can see that the *good old days* had some benefits and some liabilities.

What were the factors in the *good old days* which provided children with opportunities to develop the capabilities for living, and how can we strengthen this process today?

NOT ALL THAT WAS LOST WAS GOOD

Each of the changes outlined in the preceding chapter, which eliminated opportunities for young people to develop capabilities, were like grains of sand shifting from the positive side of the scale to the negative side. By decreasing the positive side and increasing the weight on the negative side, soon the overall balance of the culture began to shift toward a more negative, *high risk* environment.

The good news is that a few small compensations can often restore this balance and maintain a more healthy environment. In this chapter we will look at four essential elements of culture that were compromised cumulatively and collectively by the previously noted changes and outline some of the responses that Americans are already learning to make to restore the balance.

THE FOUR FACTORS WE MUST ALLOW FOR

As a result of the changes which occurred through the *great transition*, there are four major areas for which we need to adapt and compensate to emphasize dialogue, collaboration, and basic training in capabilities for young people:

- The Absence of Networks
- The Absence of Meaningful Roles
- The Absence of On-The-Job Training For Life
- The Absence of Parenting Resources

1. *Absence of Networks*

The rapid transition discussed in the previous chapter eliminated most networks. Tragically, we began this journey of change and transition as hardy, *self reliant,* rural people who believed it was unacceptable to talk about family and personal things with strangers. But that was in a world where we had to go a long way to find a stranger. Everyone was *at least an in-law.* Today we live in a world where we must go a long way to find a relative. Today, even close neighbors are often considered strangers. We can learn to change this situation, make friends with our neighbors, and create what once happened spontaneously among extended family.

Probably our greatest barrier to moving ahead with the process of building networks is the fact that too many people still believe that people need support groups because they have problems, rather than realizing that it is the people without support groups that are most likely to have serious problems today.

It is helpful for us to get over this kind of thinking and become the kind of people who discuss and explore issues with those we work with, see at the market, and live near. We will develop a large network of resources in a very short time just by talking with people.

We are the first generation in America's modern history to try to raise and educate an entire generation of young people without any active involvement of networks of grandmas, grandpas, aunts, uncles, cousins, nephews, neighbors, in-laws, and friends. Without these networks we made the peer group the primary reference group for young people.

A primary factor in young peoples' involvement with gangs and the incredible power of the peer group as we know it tends to stem from the fact that the peer groups are the validators and support systems of most young people today. In these groups young people feel *listened to, taken seriously,* and *significant.* Outside of these groups young people often feel lonely, discounted, and inadequate in families that have not been organized in the new environment to meet their basic needs.

In the past, if young people found lecturing, explaining, and moralizing at school and at home, they could then go to cousins, aunts, uncles, grandmas, and grandpas who were committed to the same family values, came from the same belief system, and were supportive of those relationships.

If we define a network, in the most simple sense, as two or

more individuals who engage in dialogue about the world and the life they are living and occasionally collaborate to achieve some mutually desirable end, then the simplest of all networks is a friendship. Networks can go upward in complexity all the way to elaborate civil defense and military networks where people share information and data and work together to achieve some outcome.

For young people, the fundamental network of the extended family provided support, wisdom, encouragement, and understanding from others when one significant adult might be momentarily lacking in wisdom. This support was necessary for the stable development of young people.

People are basically tribal creatures. We have never done well in isolation. Human beings do well when they collaborate, teach, affirm, and encourage each other.

Historically, networks provided the forum in which we tested out and validated our roles and our assumptions and shared our collective wisdom. In that way, we learned from the experiences of others.

As we lost networks, we became more isolated. We were thrown back on our own base of experience. It became harder to have any real sense of clarity or confidence about what we were doing.

Very frequently couples turned inward on each other, hoping that their partner would offset their insecurity. This process would often erode the marriage relationship. Children frequently became objects of frustration and challenge to parents who did not have the resources to figure out what to do with them. Family stress was greatly increased.

Networks are significant and important. Since we have lost them, we must make efforts to pro-actively build networks to replace those that originally occurred spontaneously. We can build networks through such things as neighborhood crime watches, support groups, parents checking with other parents, and personal growth groups.

Through the vehicle of neighborhood crime watches, which consist of people who have declared themselves involved in what happens in their neighborhood and are willing to pro-actively talk to people, we have already done more in five or six years to curtail urban crime than we did through billions of dollars of federal and state efforts. Government efforts could not succeed until people began to say, "Since I live here, I need to be involved. I am willing to talk with people at the supermarket. I will take the time to call the parents of my childrens' friends and check things out. If I see something happening at a neighbor's home, I won't just let it go. I am willing to say something about it." This kind of concern and cooperation has had a great effect in terms of safety and stability in our neighborhoods.

It has also been very effective to form networks to help young people stay out of drugs. The National Federation of Parents for Drug Free Youth was formed in 1979 and began to encourage locally initiated awareness and networking programs. It was further highlighted and promoted by the White House through their Chemical People Series. As a result, more than ten thousand local groups actively talk, share awareness, encourage, and present programs to help and support our young people.

Over the Christmas holidays of 1984 and 1985 fewer young Americans died due to drinking than in any year since 1949. Responsibility was given to such programs as Safe Homes, Safe Rides, Chemical People groups, Families in Action, Parents Who Care, Young People for Drug Free Lives, and other networks of people collaborating and engaging in dialogue about the issues in their environment.

We can learn to call our neighbors and let them know when we are going to be away for a few days so they can keep an eye on the place. We can encourage neighbors to keep an eye out for our kids and let us know if they are sticking their necks out a little too far and getting into trouble — and promise not to sue if they let us know. We can learn to see these reports, not as criticism, but as support.

I recently had a personal experience that brought me forcefully to a realization of the importance of simply establishing an identity among the people we live with.

Recently my daughter Keri left home in the family car to run some errands. She was traveling at highway speed down a narrow road when the right front tire of the car blew out and hurled the car into a narrow bridge. The car was completely demolished. Keri was pinned in the wreckage and had sustained sufficient damage to her face and body that she was suffocating.

The first person on the scene recognized the car and knew who it belonged to because we had made it a point to visit all our neighbors on the road and introduce ourselves and our family. This person sent out a call for Keri's mother, who arrived immediately. As she looked into the wreckage she could see that her daughter was suffocating and that she was the only one there who was small enough to crawl into the wreckage to clear out Keri's air passages and keep her breathing while others carefully cut her out of the demolished car.

At the hospital Keri's mother was told that even a few more moments without oxygen would have resulted in permanent brain damage or death.

By having people who knew who we were, who our children were, and where to find us, Keri's mother was able to arrive, literally, in the nick of time. The difference between having a network in which she had an identity, and not having a network, meant the difference in Keri's life and health.

When only a few minutes determined life or death for Keri, those few minutes might have been spent finding out who she was, instead of calling her mother who was small enough and motivated enough to climb into the wreckage. Because of networking, Keri is alive today.

This experience reinforced our belief that when new children begin to associate with your children, it is important to become acquainted. Develop an identity. Let them know your phone number and where you live. Don't be afraid to go down the road and stop in at someone's home and say, "I see you are new in the neighborhood. I want to introduce myself to you and meet your children and have you meet our children."

Taking the time to meet our neighbors and build networks is an excellent insurance policy and probably the only one that will do us any good when the chips are down.

An understanding of the need for networks is now becoming apparent in many areas. Churches that once provided pastoral counseling on an individual basis as their primary family service today are open most nights of the week as community centers. In these churches we find many networks such as youth groups, Big Brothers and Big Sisters, Alcoholics Anonymous and Al-anon meetings, community forums, parenting classes, and singles groups. These churches have become a center for the extended family that today we call the community.

The importance of networking is also recognized in the business world. There are professional associations, conferences, and consultants all designed to share new understandings. It does not make sense to be resistant to this kind of networking around our families and children, which is the most important business we are in.

The equivalent of a professional organization may be a parent group that meets in a church or neighbor's home. The telephone is a great tool for networking if we will use it and not be ashamed to call another parent and say, "Since our children are spending time together, I thought it might be productive for us to talk and share a few ideas. What have you heard about the event coming up this weekend?"

It has been a great thrill to see the relationship of schools and communities shift from isolation to active collaboration in the past few years. We now have large numbers of parents and community people attending and working together in school programs. They are collaborating, building networks, comparing notes and sharing responsibilities. We are already seeing that this cooperation can have long reaching effects.

As we pro-actively build networks of support and understanding around ourselves and our children in our new urban environment, we are beginning to substantially reduce the risks of isolation.

2. *Absence of Meaningful Roles*

We are the first generation to attempt to raise and educate a whole generation of young people who do not have a significant role to play in the culture. Each year we bring well over 3 1/2 million children into the world who are not needed or even expected to be significant in the economic life of their family.

These young people are also born into a culture that no longer offers the stability of rituals, traditions, and activities that validate and reinforce their role in the culture.

From the cradle to the twentieth year of life, most children in America are told, "Keep your mouth shut. Stay out of difficulty. Get good grades. Do what we tell you. Appreciate what we do for you." They are not told, "You are absolutely critical to the survival of our family. We need you. We could not accomplish what we do without what you have to offer."

A primary reason for the decline in motivation, discipline, and achievement in schools is the incredible passivity involved. Most students have the general perception that if they do not show up, the program will go on with or with out them, one way or the other. They are not used as teacher's aides as they were in the one-room schoolhouse and are not active collaborators with their teachers in their own education.

Most of their work is the passive fulfillment of someone else's plan or idea, rather than something where they are actively needed and play an essential role. They feel their significance lies only in acquiescing to the demands and wishes of others and that there is little tolerance for their specialness.

When young people are assertive in certain areas, they are often crushed. Research shows that teachers see verbally active, assertive, creative students as a liability. They have a better time with passive, quiet, acquiescing students. Being treated as a burden or as insignificant is not a very affirming world.

THE COST

In 1985, as in every year before, the data showed that 91% of adolescents who attempted suicide did so in a period of their life when they had intense doubts about their personal significance and worth in primary relationships.

In 1940 approximately seventy percent of all babies born out of wedlock to adolescents were placed for adoption. In 1986 close to ninety-seven percent of babies born to a adolescents were kept by their mothers, 40% of whom were under sixteen years of age. Much of the incentive to keep their babies reflects the belief that motherhood gave their life focus and made them feel needed and significant. This belief is reinforced by the culture who treats an adolescent mother as a woman rather than as a child.

Adolescent sexuality has been shown increasingly to be a strategy through which young people trade off something unique to make them significant, at least temporarily, in the eyes of someone else. "It is better to be important for my body and my sexuality than to be insignificant altogether."

Today we need to pro-actively deal with our young people in ways that cause them to believe they are an asset or a resource rather than an object or recipient of our activities. We can actively organize our lives so that *children play an important, contributing role in family meetings, rituals, traditions, and class councils.*

These are critical activities which help young people find a meaningful role by feeling listened to, taken seriously, and treated as significant. They are strategies we can use now to restore a base of dialogue and collaboration between young people, their parents, their schools and their communities and to give them a very clear message that they are needed. Guidelines for rituals, traditions and family meetings will be expanded upon in subsequent chapters.

3. *Absence of On-The-Job Training*

We are the first generation of Americans to attempt to raise a whole generation of young people whose on-the-job training for life generally comes more through exposure to the media than from hands on involvement with the relevant activities that provide for their life and their lifestyle.

Generally this on-the-job training through the media is quite deficient in teaching the skills of *patience, personal initiative, hard work*, and *deferred gratification* that are critical to effective responses to chemical, sexual, social, moral, ethical, and legal challenges as they enter young adulthood. On television they see self-medication, drinking, casual sexuality, expedient acts of violence, and miraculous solutions to problems within the short time span of a commercial or a 30 minute program.

FIVE BASIC THEMES FROM THE MEDIA

We would like to expand on the five basic themes for dealing with life which are portrayed repeatedly through the media. The first theme is that drinking or substance abuse is the primary activity in productive social relationships. A popular movie recently gave the impression that even the most intelligent young people could not have a good time at a party until someone brought out marijuana and alcohol.

The second theme is that self-medication is the primary problem-solving tool to resolve and deal with pain, discomfort, or boredom.

The third theme is the acceptability of casual sexuality demonstrated in the ease with which people flow in and out of relationships.

The fourth theme is the acceptability of expedient acts of violence in the way characters lash out or show *grand gestures* toward self or others to manipulate circumstances, such as suicide threats to get attention from the family or taking someone's car when in a rush. Many television *heroes* would think nothing of breaking, entering, and taking the property of someone else as long as they believed they were caught up in some higher goal of their own.

The fifth theme is shown primarily through 12 million dollars worth of commercials which depict that patience, deferred gratification, personal initiative, and hard work are unacceptable activities to be avoided most of the time through drinking, self-medicating, or using some other product or service.

A commercial for a commonly marketed coffee continuously portrays that any stressful, real-life issue or situation, such as lack of intimacy and warmth in a marriage or insecurity about the acceptability of a home, will be cured immediately by obtaining a brand of coffee, grown in special mountains, which when brewed up and served to people makes them warm, affectionate, and accepting. Thus, the nature of intimacy, warmth, and acceptance is portrayed as accessible through a product, service, or magical intervention. Young people often believe these commercial messages and television themes.

The five general themes portrayed on television have become increasingly characteristic of young people growing up in our culture today. They then apply these same concepts to their late adolescent and early adulthood lives and precipitate many of the problems we are confronted with today.

THE PRICE OF AFFLUENCE

We, as parents often compound the problems created when young people believe the television messages by using our affluence to teach children that most of their material desires can be achieved not through hard work, but through hassling, manipulating, and wishing until we give in to whatever they want.

Dr. Bob Dupont, former head of NIDA (National Institute on Drug Abuse), speaking at the PRIDE (Parents Resources In Drug Education) conferences in Atlanta, indicated that as long as we don't introduce young people, systematically, to their role in affecting the things in their life, to the need for patience, self-discipline, and hard work in accomplishing things, we actually set them up for the appeal of drugs because drugs produce instant, miraculous results, much like hassling, manipulating, and wishing.

The results are never lasting results, but they have much higher appeal to young people when all the other ways of getting their needs met would require assertiveness, patience, hard work, and waiting awhile.

Perhaps you have never thought of yourself as an affluent parent and, therefore, think problems of affluence do not apply to you. If you have any doubts about meeting the criteria for affluence, try answering the following questions:

Do you have more than one pair of shoes? Do you have more than one choice about what you will eat for each meal? Do you have access to your own transportation? Do you have more than one set of underwear?

If you answered yes to three or more of these questions, then by the overall standards of the world, you are affluent. Fewer than 10% of all people who have ever lived have been able to answer yes to three or more of those questions at any one time in their lives.

We talk about which pair of shoes to wear when a third of

the world has never owned any and only dream of the day when that might be possible. We talk about what to eat today, when a major cross-section of the world wonders if they will eat more than once during the day and is grateful for the same thing every single day. We talk about our own transportation, even for our children, when at least half of the world still walks everywhere and can only fantasize what it might be like to have a vehicle at their disposal at some time in their lifetime.

Because these things come easily for us, we don't respect them. By providing so much for children, without teaching them a healthy respect for how these things are achieved, we might be threatening their survival through adolescence. Young people are led to believe that these things will just come, and that through their hassling, manipulating, and wishing, adults will meet their needs so they can go *first class* and have the things they want.

Many young people took this attitude of going first class without having to pay their way into the arena of chemical, sexual, moral, legal, ethical and social choices. This kind of thinking created an incredible *domestic Viet Nam* last year.

In the five years of Vietnam, about 56,000 deaths were reported. In 1985, *in just one year*, we recorded the deaths of about 53,000 adolescents in America which could be attributed, in most cases, to the lack of on-the-job training which produces the belief that things will *just work out*.

Approximately 20,000 departed accidentally, with close to 12,000 of those deaths being attributed to drinking.

7,100 adolescents are considered to have committed suicide in the United States last year (given the adjustments for under reporting, which is chronic in our figures on suicide).

About 6,000 were the victims of homicide — the highest rate of youth initiated homicide on earth. Research is indicating that a significant factor in increased homicide is the impact of heavier levels of adolescent drinking on the immature systems of the brain that would normally handle impulse control and feelings.

Approximately 3,700 were the victims of domestic violence. We believe that a large cross section of this violence was due to a lack of support systems, networks, and awareness to help with family stress.

Close to 3,200 died from the complications of pregnancy, abortion, or related health problems in early adolescent bodies that were not ready for that event.

Over 1,225,000 were reported missing last year, with over

400,000 of these adolescents missing for an extended period. By the end of the average year, of all those reported missing during that year, about 125,000 remained long-term missing individuals, and it is estimated that in a normal year about 14,000 of those are actually dead due to various events. Officially they are listed as missing and may always be listed as missing.

Add them up: 20,000, 7,100, 6,000, 3,700, 3,200, 14,000. That is approximately 53,000 young people who died in 1985, in part, due to our preoccupation with materialism at the expense of relevant, validating practice at patience, self-discipline, delayed gratification, sacrifice, and hard work that would prepare young people in small doses to understand the nature of the choices that they make.

Effective parents are not using their affluence to provide everything for their children. They are not staying up all night doing science projects so their kids can do well. Effective parents are letting their children pay the freight on little things that won't hurt them, even though it might temporarily inconvenience or upset them for a little while, and then firmly and gently helping them work out alternatives for the next time a similar problem is encountered.

On-the-job training for life must include sequentially increasing doses of patience, self-discipline, deferred gratification, personal initiative, sacrifice, and hard work.

The best way to destroy self-esteem and a sense of worth is to do too much for young people. The greatest gift of all is to help young people validate themselves as an agent in their own lives. This way we help them not only to learn to meet their own needs but to contribute meaningfully to the needs of others.

4. *Loss of Parenting Resources*

We are the first generation of Americans to attempt to raise a whole generation of children whose parenting is provided as a part-time contribution of one inexperienced, biological relative for the majority of children and two inexperienced, biological relatives working part-time with the minority of children. We no longer have the collective contribution of ten to fourteen or more mature people of all different levels working together and needing each other for support through the first eighteen years of a child's life. We have ended up with fewer people to do a critical job and fewer opportunities from our lifestyle to get the job done.

At the same time, we have more challenges as parents trying to deal with the problems young people face in our society in the form of drugs, drinking, sex, and detrimental messages from the media.

MEETING THE POTENTIAL

Every human being is born on our planet with only the potential to become the most capable creature on earth. Even an amoeba is more capable at birth to function at its full potential than a human being at birth.

All the uniquely human characteristics which have allowed human beings for centuries to rise above their parents, teachers, and their environment and to cope with change better than any organism on the planet, had to be acquired in an apprenticeship between that young human being and those ahead of him or her. When this apprenticeship is adequate, their toolbox for life, which was empty at birth, is filled with the essential tools for successful living.

In times of change, the tools in the toolbox are most critical. We have chosen to call them the *tools of the learner*. We have identified seven basic tools that are essential to the parenting process. We refer to these tools as the *significant seven*. We have outlined the *significant seven* in subsequent chapters and have made them the focus of this book.

The *significant seven*, were found by accident. We were not looking at success. We were trying to describe failure. What we found was a steadily increasing body of research and data which shows that the young person most likely to become a client of the criminal justice system, human services system, and social welfare system and the young person who falls well short of his or her potential in school is the young person with the least adequate development in these seven areas.

The young person least likely to have problems in our society is the one with the most adequate development in these seven areas. Further research has begun to show that people who are successful and outstanding in many walks of life are characterized by unusual strength and adequacy in the *significant seven*.

THE SIGNIFICANT SEVEN

On the following chart, we describe the *significant seven* as they appear in inadequate individuals at birth.

HIGH RISK INDIVIDUALS

1. *Weak* perceptions of personal capabilities.

2. *Weak* perceptions of personal significance.

3. *Weak* perceptions of personal power or influence over life.

4. *Weak* intra-personal skills.

5. *Weak* inter-personal skills.

6. *Weak* systemic skills

7. *Weak* judgmental skills.

Helping children develop these perceptions and skills is important because the characteristics of children who are *high risk* in all the problem areas of drugs, early pregnancy, delinquency, and low achievement are weak in the *significant seven*.

All children are born as *high risk*. Interestingly, research shows that people who have been unusually successful but become chemically dependent for any period of time regress in all these areas. Once they are detoxified, they have to go through a *tuning up* and rebuilding in the areas of these *significant seven* in order to remain successful.

The *significant seven* are skills that are necessary for success during our whole lifetime, but they do have to be developed, and they have to be maintained in order to enjoy continued success.

When we take the first word from each of the items listed above and substitute *strong* in place of *weak*, we have the characteristics of successful, productive, capable human beings:

LOW RISK INDIVIDUALS

1. *Strong* perceptions of personal capabilities. "I am *capable*."

2. *Strong* perceptions of significance in primary relationships. "I *contribute in meaningful ways* and I am *genuinely needed*."

3. *Strong* perceptions of personal power or influence over life. "I can *influence what happens to me*."

4. *Strong* intra-personal skills. The ability to understand personal emotions, to use that understanding to develop self-discipline and self-control, and to learn from experiences.

5. *Strong* inter-personal skills. The ability to work with others and develop friendships through communication, cooperation, negotiation, sharing, empathizing, and listening.

6. *Strong* systemic skills. The ability to respond to the limits and consequences of everyday life with responsibility, adaptability, flexibility, and integrity.

7. *Strong* judgmental skills. The ability to use wisdom and to evaluate situations according to appropriate values.

Therein lies the primary goal of the parenting and teaching process, which is to specifically convert weakness to strength in these areas so that our young people have these tools in their toolbox as they mature in life.

The many changes that we have discussed in previous chapters have contributed to an environment less adequately equipped to provide young people with opportunities to develop strength in these seven areas. However parents and teachers can learn specific skills that will compensate for many of the cultural opportunities that have been lost. We can consciously provide experiences and practice in these areas in order to adequately equip the tool boxes of youth.

The young people who believe they are incapable and insignificant and that whatever happens is beyond their control will be swept away by anything and everything. They will tend to be dysfunctional sexually, chemically, socially, legally, and educationally.

Young people who believe very strongly that they are capable of initiating learning and change in their lives, that their lives have significance, and that no matter what circumstances come at them, will ultimately have the power within them to change the circumstances or at least choose how they deal with those circumstances, will be successful in whatever they set out to do in life.

It is possible to help people develop these capabilities at any time in life, but the earlier they are developed, the more likelihood of their experiencing success and happiness and fulfillment.

In subsequent chapters we will explore a veritable shopping list of specific things that can be done to encourage the development of these beliefs and capabilities.

Chapter 3

PERCEPTION

The *significant seven* consist of three critical perceptions and four essential skills. A perception is defined as the conclusions we reach as the result of an experience we have had *after there has been time to reflect on it.* A skill is what we know how to do. Perceptions are simply a result of what we think. It takes practice to acquire a skill.

Perceptions are very powerful even though they seldom have anything to do with what is true. For example, all human beings have worth. However people who choose to think they don't have worth will feel and act as if they are worthless.

Since perception is the key to all the rest, we are devoting one chapter to this crucial basis for comprehending the unique world of each individual. At least five significant aspects of perception need to be noted and understood in order to work with people effectively:

- Perception is the key to attitudes, motivation, and behavior

- Perception is a product of four elements: Experience, Identification, Analysis, And Generalization

- Perception is cumulative

- Perception is unique

- Perception must be supported before it is challenged

As each of these aspects of perception is examined in more detail, it will become evident why a clear understanding of perception is critical to developing an understanding of ourselves and others.

1. *Perception As It Relates To Attitudes and Motivation*

If we think we can, we will. If we think we can't, we won't. The only thing standing between us and our capabilities is our perceptions of who we are and what we can do. *The New Testament* tells us, "As people perceiveth themselves in their hearts, so are they."

We sometimes believe that what we see determines what we think. The opposite is true. What we think determines what we see. Alfred Adler said, "Ideas have absolutely no meaning except the meaning we give them."

The belief that rebirth occurs any time we receive a new perception of something that is possible in our lives is the foundation philosophy of perceptual psychology. Perceptual psychology is more valid and accepted today, based on the research, than it ever has been.

There has been an evolution in psychology from the determinism of Freud, to the behaviorism of Skinner, to perceptualism by the majority of psychologists today. Each of these philosophies has validity.

The development of our present understanding of psychology actually followed the normal sequence of human development. We come into the world as creatures of instinct at birth to help us survive. We then develop conditioned responses which allow us to anticipate immediate cause and effect. And, finally we mature into perceptual human beings.

A similar sequence unfolded in the development of Judeo/Christian reasoning. The stimulus-response Law of Moses was a schoolmaster philosophy of "Do this or else." From the Christian perspective, The Sermon On The Mount raised people to a more volitional level. This transition suggests that the higher order reasoning of the human race is to do things volitionally, out of understanding and belief, rather than out of fear of punishment or habit.

We believe that perceptual psychology is the most human and the most humane, as well as the most dynamic and optimistic of psychologies. We applaud the research and the data that points this way. The focus of this book is to help adults find more effective ways of working with young people based on an understanding of perceptual psychology.

As normally developing human beings pass the age of eight, they increasingly become creatures of perception. From that point on, their perception is the key to what they are and what they do. They can revise their history, change their present, and transcend their parents and teachers by changing their perceptions.

To try changing the behavior of others without changing their perceptions only opens the door to new behavior that will manifest the existing perception.

For a number of years we have tried to intervene in the problems of young people by encouraging their skill development, such as communications skills and problem-solving skills. This approach has proven ineffective because these young people would be sent back into environments where their interaction with adults reinforced negative perceptions of "Why try? They won't give me a chance anyway. There is nothing I can do. Everything is fate or luck anyway." Without perceptual change, people are not motivated to use skills in new ways.

So, our first task is to be sure the environment in which we work with young people cultivates perceptions of capability. Adults who work with young people need to understand perceptions, how they are developed, and how they are changed.

All human beings have a basic need for potency, for a sense of control over their environment, for appreciation for their perceptions and feelings, and for significance. When these basic needs are blocked, people experience frustration.

When people are frustrated, they have three choices. Strong, confident people confront the situation and change things. Less confident people, having that avenue closed because of perceptions of fear or inadequacy, have two choice left: 1) fight their frustration through rebellion and resistance, or 2) flee into depression, withdrawal, and passivity.

It is important for us to remember that perception is the key to attitude, motivation and behavior. If we don't change perceptions, we will get only temporary change in behaviors, attitudes, and motivation, or displacement of those into other areas.

Whenever we see behaviors, attitudes, and motivations that are a concern to us, particularly in young people, we must spend enough time studying them to find out where in their life their basic needs are being frustrated. Then if we can't change the conditions, we must work to change their perceptions about them.

2. *Perception Is The Product Of Four Elements*

Experience
Identification
Analysis
Generalization

When learning passes through these four levels, it becomes a permanent part of the way we see the world:

The *experience* itself, which can come in many forms.

What we *identify* as significant in that experience.

Our *analysis* based on our rationale for why it is significant.

The *generalization* that comes from our unique perceptions of what possible value the experience has for us.

Professionals in the field of training have developed the EIAG acronym to help them remember this process of experience, identify, analyze, and generalize. If this seems a little hard to remember, we can think of it as the *What? Why? and How?* process.

The EIAG (*What? Why? How?*) process greatly enhances dialogue and strengthens relationships between adults and children *when done in a climate of genuine interest and support.*

We cannot stress too much how important it is to convey an attitude of friendliness and unconditional acceptance when pursuing this process as follows:

1. Experience: Become aware of experiences in the lives of young people — either negative or positive.

2. Identify: Help them identify the significant elements or outcomes of the event. "What happened? What did you see? What are you feeling? What was the most important thing?"

3. Analyze: Help them analyze why the aspects of the event were important. "Why was that significant to you? Why do you think it happened? Since children are used to the *why* question being used against them, it might be less threatening to rephrase these questions as follows: What made that seem important to you? What were you trying to do? What caused you to feel that way?"

4. Generalize: Help them generalize a single principle that can be used in similar situations. "How can you use this information in the future? How can you do it differently next time for different results? What do you need to repeat if you want to achieve similar results again?"

Whenever we explore these four elements, we also affirm

and validate people's perceptions. One of the most common errors in working with young people is to assume that they understand and interpret what they experience the same as a mature person does.

When we use the EIAG process, whether it is in the classroom, the home, in counseling, or in personal relationships, we help young people personalize their life experiences and develop their perceptions. We also begin to understand *how* they interpret different events. This process also helps us avoid the *barrier of assuming*, which will be discussed later.

One of the authors tells the following story about an experience with his young son, who was 10 years old at the time, which exemplifies this process rather clearly:

MICHAEL AND THE TRACTOR

Because I travel a great deal, I go out of my way to find opportunities for Michael to do things with me when I am home. My goal in that process is to help him perceive himself as significant and as contributing meaningfully to what we do together. One of my strategies recently was to ask for his assistance in fixing a tractor.

The tie-rod had broken and required welding. I outfitted Michael with some leather gloves and a welding mask so he could hold the parts in alignment while I did the welding.

After we had finished the welding and I began to put the tools away, Michael said, "Thanks, Dad, for letting me help you fix the tractor."

I reflected on his statement. It was obvious that he appreciated the opportunity, but a perceptive listener would recognize that I had not achieved my goal of helping Michael believe that he had done something important for me. He was indicating his belief that I had done something important for him. In order to help him understand the importance of his role, I knew that I needed to check out his perception of the experience and then help him re-evaluate.

I reflected back what I had heard, "Michael, I appreciate the fact that you thanked me for letting you help me fix the tractor, but that also says to me that you may not understand that I could not have fixed the tractor without you.

His immediate response was, "Sure you could, Dad. You can do anything."

I had forgotten what it means to be six years old and to look at your father, who solves all the problems and fixes everything. What does a six-year-old believe his father could not do without him? From his point of view I am as potent as the Dukes of Hazzard, who can do anything. So, I said, "Son, I appreciate your confidence in me, but there are some things that I can't do without your help, and this was one of them."

He asked, "What do you mean, Dad?" Now he was more interested.

I reflected the question back, "Why do you believe I could not have fixed the tractor without you?" At age six, I know that question is probably at a higher level than he is ready for, but how do I know what he is ready for if I don't check periodically?

I started a little high by asking him to analyze the situation and tell me what he thought.

He was not defensive, but expressed genuine confusion when he said, "I don't know."

I followed with an easier, *describe* question. Small children can often describe, but not interpret. We can usually build an interpretation out of a description. So, my next question was, "Well, what was it you had to do?"

He understood that question. "I had to hold the tie-rod together."

I said, "And, what was it that I had to do?"

He said, "You had to do the welding."

I asked, "How many hands did it take to keep the tie-rod lined up?"

He said, "Two."

"And how many hands did it take to do the welding?"

He said, "Two."

"Well, if it takes two hands to hold the tie-rod, and two hands to weld it, how many hands does it take to fix the tractor?"

He said, "Does math have something to do with it?"

Up until that time I am sure he believed that math was something we used to persecute small children with homework. But suddenly it took on enormous significance if it could fix a tractor, which was more relevant in his eyes.

He brightened up and said, "It takes four."

I said, "Well, if it takes four hands to do the job, how many do you have?"

He said, "Two."

"How many do I have?"

"Two."

I said, "Could either of us have done this job alone?"

He said, "No way, Dad."

He was excited now and asked, "Why does the tractor keep breaking in the first place?"

I said, "Well, Son, when I am out doing the bush hogging and I am driving along watching where the bush hog is going, I don't always see stumps in the grass. When the tractor hits them, sometimes they break the tie-rod."

He said, "Well, Dad, just like it takes four hands to fix the tractor, doesn't it take four eyes to drive it?"

I was overwhelmed with his insight. I contemplated for a moment and said, "You are right."

He said, "Well, just like I helped you fix it, I could probably help you keep from breaking it. But not if I have to sit back where you sit. I couldn't see the stumps either."

I asked, "What would we have to do so you could help me?"

He said, "We would have to build a seat and put it up here on the front so I could watch for the stumps."

So we built a seat, put a little seat belt on it, and fastened it on the front. Now as we drive along, he yells, "Stump!" and I turn around it. It has been two years, and we haven't broken the tractor once.

If you visit our ranch, Michael will tell you very quickly, "Dad used to break the tractor all the time until I took responsibility for the stumps."

Since that time I haven't very often come home when Michael hasn't met me with a list of things that need fixing on the ranch, tasks that take two people. What he learned from the tractor experience is that when it takes two, "I am sometimes equal to my father, and that makes me very significant."

His learning continued. A few weeks later I received a call from his teacher who asked, "What have you been doing to Michael?"

I asked, "Why do you ask?"

She said, "Well, he used to just sit there, waiting for instructions. Now he is going around offering suggestions and helping people. Couldn't we go back to when he used to just sit there?"

I replied, "Well, look at it this way. It is easier to tame a fanatic than to put life into a corpse. Now that he believes he is important, he is looking around for opportunities to help. That is a whole lot better than having him sitting in the back, distracted and uninterested in what is going on. Why don't you see if you can develop a plan to utilize a six-year-old teacher's aide? You might, for example, tell him, 'Michael, I appreciate your help so much, but there are times when I need to do things with the class myself.' So I will tell you, 'This is my time, Mike. If you want to help, listen thoughtfully and carefully. When you are ready to help, I will come over and test you out to see if you have got it. If you have it, then you can go around and be helpful to others.'"

He is a little man who is now motivated by the prospects of being able to help. He sits in the corner of the classroom, listening intently, and often asks, "Are you done yet? Check me out. I've got it."

If we go back and look at that episode, the experience itself was being involved in fixing the tractor. Had I left it there, I have no doubt that Michael would not have seen himself as any more significant afterward than he did before. But when I explored what was significant in that experience as he understood it, why it was a significant contribution, and how he could learn from that experience to affect other things in his life, then he had it. His perception had changed: "When I can find someplace where my efforts are needed and important, I am significant."

The difference between fixing the tractor and the perception of personal significance lay in taking the three steps beyond the experience.

IT IS NATURAL

Some people feel intimidated by the EIAG process and claim it feels unnatural to stop and ask the What? Why? How? questions in a climate of friendly support.

However, we use this process everyday without thinking about it. Suppose you have been wanting a Weedeater but hesitated to buy one because you thought it was too expensive. Then you notice an ad in the newspaper for Weedeaters on sale. As you scan the ad, *what* is important in the ad for you? The Weedeater. *Why* is it important? Because you need one and the price is good. Immediately your mind searches for *how* you can respond, and you begin to develop a plan to get to the store to purchase the Weedeater.

Every significant thing we have ever learned in our lives has come through this process. Because it is subtle, like breathing, we are most often not even aware of it.

We do not need to struggle with this process, but we need to be aware of its importance for real learning to take place. It is not important to go through every step every time. It is important to develop an *awareness* that the perceptions of others are different than our own and to develop an *attitude* and *interest* in exploring the perceptions of young people to help them internalize an awareness of their capabilities.

MISUSE

We misuse the EIAG process when we use it to manipulate people into disregarding their own perceptions and accepting ours as the *correct* way to see things. This use is inappropriate. This process should be used only with a genuine attempt to explore the perceptions of others. When this is our goal, the process comes easily. The words are simply *what, why or in what way, and how.* When we more consciously think this way, with an attitude of genuine interest in the unique world of others, we will be more facilitative in working with people.

KEEP THE SPIRIT

One workshop participant shared that she had difficulty with the *what, why and how* process, and that her child would still respond with, "I don't know."

One of the authors was able to share what she had learned from a similar experience:

I had the same problem with my first attempts at this process with my son, Mark. I learned that my first problem was *losing the spirit or purpose* of the process to really explore his perceptions and was focusing on how proficient I could be with the *technique.* I was more interested in being *right* than in getting into his world.

Even more important was the advice I received from Steve to stop trying anything until I had learned to be a *closet listener.* When I quit focusing on myself and became quiet enough to give Mark a chance to talk at his own pace, I was amazed at how much he started opening up and sharing things of interest to him. He even shared a few feelings when I simply conveyed a quiet attitude of interest and was *patient.*

CLOSET LISTENING

A *closet listener* will simply avoid trying to force the communication process at first and just pay attention to what is actually going on. People communicate a great deal with their silences, with their attitude, with where they choose to be or not to be, or with their posture. People tend to clam up when we push a process that has been threatening.

One mother arrived home from a workshop with great enthusiasm. She went straight to her teenager's room and said, "Is their anything that you need to communicate to me?" This traumatized the whole system.

Think back to when you were a teenager. What are the implications of a question like that? "Did she find my stash? Did she go through my wallet and find incriminating evidence? Did she see me someplace I should not have been? Does she have a specific answer in mind?"

Most young people believe that the safest response to questions from adults is, "I don't know."

We reduce the threat when we pay attention to people without letting them know we are doing it. Sometimes it helps to forget about the *What? Why? and How?* questions and focus instead on an attitude of genuine interest until the questions come naturally from the feeling generated by that attitude.

When we patiently explore the *What?* the *Why?* and the *How?* with people, not to manipulate them into coming up with what we want but to genuinely share the process of discovery with them, then we can help them take meaning from their experience and build their confidence as they think things through. We must remember that it is not the event but how the person interprets the event that determines what they perceive about it.

The EIAG process takes a little more time and a little more collaboration, so it has largely been eliminated from the normal home and classroom setting. Yet it is essential for critical thinking, moral and ethical development, comprehension, and wisdom. We are struggling in all those areas in our culture. The more we can be patient with this process ourselves and use it to increase dialogue with our children, the more we can prepare them to offset the lack of dialogue they are likely to encounter it in our crowded classrooms.

3. *Perception Is Cumulative*

The third element is that perception is cumulative. Most of us have had the experience of reading a book at one time and then re-reading it at a later time and discovering significant new insights.

We tend to grow, as the *Bible* says, line upon line, and precept upon precept. People who are threatened in various ways in the learning environment tend to clam up and remain at the same level if not given room to grow in small, cumulative steps.

We have forgotten about the concepts of perception when we ask, "How many times do I have to tell you? Surely you realize! Why don't you think? You are old enough to understand!" These judgments we tend to make indicate that we are not paying attention to the fact that perception is cumulative and that people must go from their present level to the next level in an environment of encouragement. We often expect people to have knowledge they have not had a chance to encounter and assimilate.

Instead of confronting young people with their inadequacy, we should take steps to help them accumulate more wisdom with respect for individual rates of understanding.

DON'T DWELL ON GUILT

There are probably not many parents alive today, including the authors, who will not feel some pangs of guilt when reading the above comments. Throughout this book we will stress that we are not talking about perfection, but about awareness and small steps toward improvement.

Guilt is useless if it lasts longer than ten seconds. In ten seconds we can use our feelings of remorse as an indicator of ineffective behavior. That is the time to simply start over. Some of us have to start over many times, and sometimes we have to wait until we have calmed down and then start over. This will be discussed in Chapter 11 under the heading of *Recovery*.

WISDOM DEVELOPS NATURALLY IN CLIMATES OF SUPPORT

We need patience with ourselves and our young people. The one thing we cannot transfer to our children, ever, is wisdom. They have to accumulate it for themselves. We can help them accumulate it, but we can never transfer wisdom by demanding and threatening.

Mark Twain understood this process when he said, "When I was 14 it seemed to me that my parents did not know anything. By the time I was 21, I was impressed at how much they had learned."

We won't be so frustrated when young people are not impressed with our wisdom if we remember that it is normal for them to go through a *know it all* stage during adolescence while exploring their own perceptions and values. During this period it is very important to take time and use dialogue to explore the perceptions they are accumulating. Otherwise, the last person they want emulate is their parents who are always demanding and expecting things they don't have.

4. *Perception Is Unique*

The following is a very popular quote by an unknown author:

"I know you believe you understand what you think
I said. But, I am not sure you realize that what you
heard is not what I meant."

The greatest lie ever told by the human race is, "I know just what you mean." That is absolutely impossible because people's perceptions are more unique than their finger prints.

No two people have ever read the same book. Nor has anyone ever read the book that the author actually wrote. Teachers make a mistake when they ask, "What was the most important thing the author was emphasizing?" rather than, "What was your perception of what was important in the book?"

One of the authors is large, bearded, and bald-headed and has made the statement that "Every book I ever read had a bearded, bald guy for a hero."

The other author sees it differently and says, "I always thought the hero looked more like Robert Redford."

The first author finds that perception quite incredible. "I always picture Robert Redford playing the villain. I guess that is why I always feel ripped off when I go to a movie and see my favorite books messed up that way. I always find they put a bald guy in the role of the villain, and the hero always looks more like Robert Redford or Tom Selleck, and that is just not the way the book worked out for me."

Each of us, in reading a book, has a unique experience based upon our unique perception. That is why no two people have ever read the same book. Reading a book is our own unique fantasy, and we see in it what we are prepared to see.

When authors write books they are attempting to record their perceptions. When people interpret books, they pass them through their perceptions and add different emphasis and meaning.

With this understanding we must remember that the least effective role for us as parents and teachers is the time we spend explaining our perceptions rather than exploring the perceptions of young people as we try to teach something. The point was illustrated beautifully by the following story:

A mother and father had gone away for the weekend and left their two children with a babysitter. On the Friday before they left, the had been to a doctor and learned that their 5-year-old son need to have his tonsils removed.

While they were gone, this boy decided to hasten the process along. He removed the spring from his little hobby horse and twisted it firmly into his throat in an attempt remove his tonsils. The babysitter had to rush him to the emergency room at the hospital to have the spring removed from his throat.

The mother was very upset about this incident. When talking with the boy later, she pointed out, "That was a very silly thing to do, wasn't it honey, to put that spring down your throat? See all the pain it caused you."

The little boy said, "No Mom, it wasn't silly."

Mom insisted, "Honey, it really was. It was a very silly thing to do."

The little boy insisted, "No, it wasn't silly, Mom."

Finally a little bell rang in her head and she realized she was assuming the child's perceptions were the same as hers. She stopped and asked, "Honey, what does silly mean to you?"

He answered, "Something that you laugh at, and this was nothing to laugh at, Mom. It really hurt my throat."

The English language usually offers several meanings for each word. To achieve understanding, we have to consider words in context and do quite a bit of negotiating through dialogue to achieve clarity of another person's perception.

NO TWO ALIKE

From the moment two identical twins are laid in their bassinet, they record different experiences each moment. One may see shadows. One may see light. Even when they see the same things, they each bring their unique interpretation through which to experience each event.

If Adam and Eve had spent more time in dialogue with Cain and Abel individually, they might have detected that Abel's perceptions were not the same as Cain's and perhaps might have taken some steps to correct misunderstandings. At least they left behind a legacy that let us know how they tried, what they learned, and their hope for us to do better.

We can never assume than any two children or any two adults will see the same event in the same way. That is why it is important to become more committed to dialogue. We don't know how young people interpret their experiences, and sometimes they are not sure how to interpret their experiences until we explore them together in a climate of support.

Whenever we try to rush this process, whenever we demand more experience than people have had a chance to gather, then we tend to intimidate them and help them accumulate the perception of inadequacy, rather than clear perceptions of the situation.

5. *Perception Grows In A Climate Of Support And Challenge*

Support must precede a challenge when we want to motivate others to change. When we are challenged in an environment where we don't feel supported, then all our energy goes into defending ourselves. That energy could go into learning and changing when the situation is not threatening.

The following Barriers and Builders to creating a climate of support are themes expressed throughout the book.

BARRIERS THAT MAKE INTERACTIONS THREATENING

1. Unwillingness to consider the validity of another person's point of view.

2. Discounting or judging another person's point of view.

3. Blaming others for personal feelings, "You make me angry."

4. A lack of genuineness indicated by a tone of voice that implies the opposite of what we are saying.

BUILDERS TO CREATE A CLIMATE OF SUPPORT

1. Openness to exploring another person's point of view

2. Listening to understand another person's point of view.

3. Empathy that can come only after true listening.

4. Genuineness which is conveyed through warmth and interest.

5. Ownership for personal feelings.

6. Respect for differing points of view.

It does not work to say, "That is ridiculous; you know I love you." Right up front the message of love is destroyed when we are discounting rather than supportive.

When we are truly loving, we don't see the perceptions of others as ridiculous. We seek understanding with, "Honey, let me be sure I understand what caused you to see in that way." This attitude is supportive and can be followed with a loving challenge, "Now that I understand, I would like you to reconsider this assumption."

We can see the difference. One response is supportive and shows a genuine desire to explore perceptions. The other response is discounting and non-supportive demonstrated by judging and *putting down* the perception of a *loved* one.

The EIAG process, discussed earlier in this chapter, will help us avoid the barriers. It is a supportive process which helps us accumulate the insight that is necessary to explore another person's unique point of view. For this reason, and many others that will become apparent, we will emphasize the EIAG process throughout our explorations together.

In subsequent chapters we will discuss more steps we can take to help our young people accumulate a unique understanding of their capabilities and their significance and their potency in a climate of support and challenge.

Chapter 4

DEVELOPING STRONG PERCEPTIONS OF PERSONAL CAPABILITIES

An essential building block of success is a belief in personal capabilities. The first of the *significant seven* deals with this issue.

Children find in the eyes of the parents and teachers who raise and educate them, mirrors in which they discover themselves. This beautiful statement expresses one of the most important principles for helping children learn to see themselves as capable people. It is easiest to gain this belief when they spend time with people who believe they are capable and who treat them that way.

Children are motivated to learn and do things from birth and usually see themselves as capable at a very young age. When Scott was eighteen months old, he would constantly pester his mother to let him help. "Me do it," he would declare enthusiastically as he would follow her around the house. He wanted to push the vacuum, dust the furniture, crack the eggs, and help with all the cooking.

"No, honey. You are too little to help me now. Go play with your toys or watch TV now."

Mom had started the process of altering Scott's feelings of capability very early. Scott learned his lessons well. When he was ten-years-old, Mom would say, "Come into the kitchen and set the table."

Scott would either ignore her or reply, "I'm busy playing with my toys, Mom." Mom didn't realize he was only doing what he had been trained to do. She would be upset and frustrated.

SEE CHILDREN AS CAPABLE PEOPLE

Children naturally want to help and to feel needed. They want to do *important* jobs. True a small child cannot vacuum or scramble eggs as well as an adult, but with training they can do an adequate job. Besides, a job well done is not as important as helping a child develop skills and capabilities.

Some parents may object, "But my three-year-old child might burn herself if I let her scramble the eggs."

This is true, but the chances of a burned finger are quite small if a parent has taken time to teach the child how to scramble the eggs and has used the EIAG process to explore the child's understanding of what could happen if he touches the hot stove or pan, why it would happen, and how to make sure it does not happen. It is also true that a small burn is not as harmful to a child as the damage that is done when feelings of capability are lost.

TAKE TIME FOR TRAINING

We can take time to train children and then let them scramble the eggs, dust the furniture, unload the dishwasher, help with the shopping, and contribute in other meaningful ways. When we appreciate their contributions, no matter how small, we help them continue seeing themselves as capable.

AVOID BARRIERS AND USE BUILDERS

We have identified five behaviors that occur with great consistency in almost all relationships between the more mature and less mature, which express a disbelief in the capabilities of the less mature person, and which often begin to create barriers to growth and barriers to closeness and trust.

We have also identified five alternate behaviors that can be learned and substituted, which consistently affirm and validate other people and our belief in their capabilities.

We are going to emphasize, as we go through these barriers and builders, first the negative, because that is the most common.

WHEN NOTHING IS BETTER THAN SOMETHING

Each barrier behavior lowers the capacity of a relationship to support, affirm, and encourage people and tends to reduce the belief in one's capabilities. *When we do nothing more than eliminate these barriers, we experience a substantial improvement in all our relationships with people, particulary with children.*

WHEN SOMETHING IS BETTER THAN NOTHING

We will enjoy a 200% improvement in strong relationships with our children when each barrier is replaced by the five builders.

Each of the barrier behaviors reduces peoples' belief in their capabilities or eliminates a chance to gain experience. Each of the builders promotes a belief in capabilities.

BARRIER NO. 1 — ASSUMING

The barrier of assuming is generally borne out of expediency. It is very tempting to be quick to assume what those we love and live with will or won't do or how they are or aren't going to respond, and then deal with them according to our assumptions. Have you said to someone, "I didn't tell you because you always get so upset." Then you were surprised that they got upset for not being allowed to try not to get upset.

When I go home, my mother says, "Don't forget your coat." I forgot it when I was eight. She is convinced there has been no growth in 37 years. Have you ever noticed how people regress when they go home because of this history of past assumptions?

If Helen Keller had been left at home with people to do everything for her, she would have lived a very limited life because her family had already assumed what people with her impairments could not do. It wasn't until someone refused to accept these assumptions and give her a chance to try, instead of *assume it away*, that her potential was unblocked.

When we assume, we ignore the most beautiful characteristic of human beings, which is the ability to learn and change from day to day. By assuming, we say, "What you were yesterday is all I will allow you to be today."

B. F. Skinner, the famous psychologist, showed that creatures such as rats respond to the same stimulus the same way over and over out of habit or instinct, but human beings respond based on beliefs. When a stimulus comes to the attention of a human brain, it passes through a belief system at that time and produces a *menu* of possible responses.

The brain then looks over the menu and, based on the person's beliefs at that moment, selects or creates a behavior. However, as people proceed with the behaviors they learn from each experience and change their beliefs, the next day the same stimulus may produce a different response.

For example, a spark pops out of the fireplace, and I rush over and step on it with my bare foot. Next time I will probably try a broom or water.

If we want people to believe that they can grow and change, then I have to allow for it in our relationships.

Perhaps a good question to ask before we assume is, "What would happen if I don't assume?" The answer is that we would find out! Whenever possible it is better to do nothing and find out than to assume prematurely and be the last to grow and encourage.

I have this fantasy of my mother deciding to be quiet when she sees me walk toward the door, instead of assuming I will forget my coat. I would probably get to the doorway and say, "Aren't you going to remind me of my coat?"

She would say, "No, Dear, I'm sure if it is important to you, you'll get it." Then I can say, "Well, I'd better get it because it could get cold out there." And she will be able to see that in 37 years I have finally caught on.

BUILDER NO. 1 — CHECKING

Checking is a way to learn about the understanding and capability of our children and to help them develop their perceptions and discover their capabilities.

Mom could have said, "Honey, what kinds of things will you need to have ready before you go out? What about the weather?"

When we check it out, we are saying we respect the fact that people are growing and changing, and we are trying to make room for it.

These principles also apply with spouses and all family relationships. When we assume what a spouse will or won't do, "I didn't tell you about it because you always get so annoyed," that assumption is disrespectful and always leads to anger and frustration. It is better to substitute assuming with, "Honey, I need to check something out with you. I know these events usually upset you, but I felt we had better discuss it." That approach at least gives the spouse a chance to try.

When possible we can substitute dialogue and patience for assuming: "How can I use this situation to check out what this person knows, sees, is ready to learn, or can do?"

BARRIER NO. 2 — RESCUING/EXPLAINING

Parents and teachers often rescue children instead of allowing them to experience the consequence of their behavior. Or, we step in and explain things instead of helping children discover what happened.

There is a prevailing belief that good parents and teachers *explain* lots of things to children. However, truly effective parents and teachers work with children to help them develop useful explanations for themselves. Explaining is often confusing. Think of it yourself. Have you ever had people start explaining something to you that they were quite familiar with, but you had never thought through before? The longer they went on with the explanation, the more confused and frustrated you became.

There comes a time when they have to stop and say, "What is your understanding of what I have tried to explain so far?" As they feed back their understanding, you can see what they understand and where they are still confused. Then input can be helpful when they are actively involved in thinking it through. It is less helpful when they haven't given you that chance.

Children feel intimidated whenever we are too quick to step in and take care of something for them or too quick to step in and explain things for them. Our *brilliance* baffles them and leaves them feeling very vulnerable to what would happen if we were not there.

People who step in too quickly to take care of things for others are called rescuers and enablers. They rescue people from their inadequacy and then enable them to remain vulnerable and easily manipulated.

It happens all the time. I hear it at my neighbor's house: "This is what happened." "This is why it happened." "This is what you better do to fix it." These statements imply, "Shut up, dummy. If you would let others do things for you, you wouldn't be such a mess in the first place." These statements do not encourage children to know that they are capable and significant.

I have talked with many newly married couples who acknowledged their fear and uncertainty at suddenly being expected to begin budgeting, shopping, arranging health care, shelter, and doing all the many things that had always been done for them at home.

By stepping in too quickly to take care of something for others, we prevent the necessary experience from developing. Then by stepping in too quickly to explain, instead of being patient and inviting them to think it through without a put-down, we prevent the growth even when they did have the experience. In either case, *doing nothing, patiently*, is far better and far more helpful than *doing something prematurely that discounts the person*.

BUILDER NO. 2 - EXPLORING

When we explore the *What? the Why? and the How?* of an experience, to learn how it was perceived in the mind of the person who has had the experience, we respect the four elements of perception that we mentioned earlier in this chapter. We need to allow children to have the experience, and then instead of explaining to them what happened and why it happened and how it happened and telling them what they need to do to fix it, it is more effective to explore those concepts with them:

"What is your understanding of what was happening or going on? What might have caused that to happen? Having had that experience, what could you learn from it that might help you next time?"

When we are patient in exploring with young people, we are saying, "I see within you the capabilities to master situations and gain understanding. And, rather than pre-empt you with my impatience, I will take the time to work with you on your discoveries," as in the following example.

Mary forgot her lunch. The school secretary allowed her to use the phone to call and ask her mother to bring it to school. When Mary's mother refused to bring her lunch to school, the school staff felt she was very cruel and irresponsible.

Mary's mother was not interested in demonstrating her responsibility. She was interested in helping Mary learn from her experiences and gave the school permission to let Mary walk home to get her lunch.

Mary also was angry with her mother for *making* her walk home. Her mother put her lunch by the front door and got into the shower. When Mary marched into the bathroom, ready to express her anger and to try manipulating her mother into taking her back to school in the car, her Mom said, "Honey, I'm busy now. You'll need to hurry back to school. We can talk about it later."

After school, when Mom knew Mary had been able to *cool off* somewhat, she listened to Mary express how embarrassed she had been because her mother would not bring her lunch to school. Then she asked Mary, "Do you know I really love you?"

Mary admitted that she did. Then her Mom asked, "Do you know I really want what is best for you?"

Mary said, "It doesn't seem like you care when you won't bring my lunch to school for me when I forget it."

Mom said, "Honey, let's take a look at that. What happened to cause you to forget your lunch?"

Mary said, "I was in such a rush to catch the bus that I just forgot it."

"How did you feel about not having your lunch?"

Mary admitted, "It wasn't so bad. Other kids loaned me things from their lunches, but it is better to have my own."

Mom asked, "What do you think you could learn from that if you want to remember your lunch in the future?"

Mary said, "Well, one thing I learned is that you won't bring it for me because you want me to be more responsible. What a drag! I Suppose I could leave my lunch by the front door so I can grab it when I'm in a rush."

"Can you think of anything else?"

Mary thought a minute and said, "Well, I could also get up as soon as my alarm rings so I won't be so rushed."

Mom joked, "Did you think I would deprive you of all that learning by bringing your lunch for you?"

LEARNING FROM EXPERIENCES

When children are about to go out to play and it is not an extremely cold day and they have not had a significant illness, if they go out without their jacket, all that will happen is that they will get uncomfortable. A wise parent will let children learn from their experiences. A rescuing parent will say, "Be sure and put on your jacket, dear. It is very cold out there." If the child went out without the jacket and came in cold, the explaining parent might make the mistake of saying, "Now you know that you shouldn't be out there when it is cold. That was a silly thing to do." Those are discouraging comments.

Encouraging parents allow their children to go out without their jackets. When they come in and say, "Mom, I am cold," instead of saying, "No wonder, Dummy, you forgot your jacket," they will explore. "Yesterday you were out playing and you weren't cold. What was different?"

"Yesterday I had a jacket, and a hat, and gloves. Today I ran out in my t-shirt."

"If you want to keep playing out there without being cold, what things could you do."

"Well, I guess I could get my jacket."

"Okay. It is up to you, honey, if you want to be warm."

One mother shared that she had never had much luck convincing her child to save her allowance for future desires during the week. She would try explaining to Lisa that she would be sorry later if she spent it all the first day. Lisa would still spend it all early. Then her mother would explain, "I told you so. Why don't you ever listen?" Every week would be a repeat of the same thing.

The mother was surprised at how little it took to get different results. The next allowance day, when Lisa wanted to spend her money on a snowcone, Mom asked, "How do you think you will feel tomorrow when your money is gone? Can you think of anything else you might want to have money for during the rest of the week?"

She was amazed when Lisa simply said, "I guess I don't really want the snowcone. I'm sure I will want something more during the week."

This mother said, "I felt awkward asking these questions, and I wasn't even patient enough to wait for a response to my first question, but I started the process, and it encouraged Lisa to think for herself instead of asserting her independence by rebelling against my attempts to explain and rescue her from making mistakes."

Using this *builder* helps children develop judgement by teaching them to learn from their experiences. By *rescuing* and *explaining* we retard judgmental maturity, in addition to reducing a sense of their capabilities.

BARRIER NO. 3 — DIRECTING

Directing is another of the behaviors most likely to be borne out of expediency. It is so much easier to step in and make sure things are done our way than to invite the participation of our children and accept that sometimes they will do things a little differently. Human beings are basically very independent creatures who demand a certain level of respect for their uniqueness. When we are too quick to step in an direct, we produce hostility, aggression, and resistance.

How do we feel when supervisors or bosses insist on telling us every detail of a task that we are supposed to understand? We usually feel discounted and insignificant. If they do it long enough, we will look for another job, or our motivation and our willingness to cooperate will drop off sharply. When they invite our contributions with respect, we believe that they feel we have something to offer.

Directing creates an enormous barrier. Most of us know better that to use *directing, but we might hear a neighbor say to a child, "Pick that up. Put that away. It is time for your shower. Be sure and drink your milk before the bus comes." Invariably we also hear later, "Dummy, you took your shoes but you left your socks."*

That is how kids get even: "You didn't say socks." They can make us feel frustrated and impotent, just as they felt, by resisting or refusing to do every detail our way.

They will often go out of their way to change, even slightly, what we required them to do, just to assert their independence.

Directing is a significant barrier that affects family life and is probably one of the most widespread of the negative barriers we see because it is *easier to do it myself* than to invite contribution and cooperation. On the other hand, whenever we can find the patience to invite and encourage people's participation, we can say to our kids, "Listen, I have some friends coming, and the family room is a mess. If you could get it straightened up for me, it would really help me out a lot." Then they will take their socks and their shoes and get the room pretty straight.

Many parents and teachers *direct* children through each step, instead of *exploring* how a task could be accomplished.

Instead of saying, "Honey, you will need to check the time," which is a *directing* response, a better response would be, "What time do you need to be ready to leave? Is there anything you will need my help with in getting ready?"

Directing makes children feel impotent and frustrated. The more directive a parent or teacher is, the more rebellious and resistant children become.

One workshop participant shared with the group what happened to her during the three day training program: "I always leave these lists of instructions for my husband and children and come home and find them resentful and the instructions only half way followed. I could not understand why they always seemed hostile when I came home and left things on the list only partially done."

She got caught up in the training and became so enthused that she stayed up all night preparing for the first unit. In the morning she was re-checking and lost track of time. All of a sudden she realized she was going to be late. As she ran out the door, she said to her husband, "I have been real caught up in this training. I haven't had a chance to organize anything, and we have company coming tonight. If you get home before I do, I would appreciate anything you could do to help me out."

When she came home, food was cooking on the stove, the washing machine was going downstairs, and her husband was vacuuming in the family room.

She said, "What's happened?

He said, "I knew you were in difficulty because you didn't have time to leave one of those damn lists I hate so much. As I've been vacuuming, I've been thinking, and it occurred to me that I lived thirty years successfully before we married. I paid my bills, took care of the things I needed to do, entertained my friends, and organized my life, and I haven't received much credit for that since we married. I was beginning to get in touch with how much I am beginning to feel towards you the way I felt toward my mother when she did this to me. I finally left her for another woman."

They were in the kind of trouble which is born out in research showing that whichever spouse adopts a directing role over the other one generally promotes in the other one the rationale or incentive for outside relationships or burying himself or herself in his or her work where he or she feels more equal and accepted.

ADULTS ARE ALSO RESISTANT TO DIRECTING

We worked with a staff development coordinator for a major school district who was so limiting, controlling and directing that she constantly reduced everyone in the system to a level of kindergarten children. Their behavior toward her showed that resentment. We came to the end of the first day, and she said, "I want each of you to pick up your cup and put it in this trash can before you go." One-third of them left their cups right where they were. They were principals, superintendents, and other people used to having some authority, and they resented her behavior.

The next day, we stepped in to demonstrate what her directing behavior was costing her. We said, "The school is going to have another meeting in here when this one is finished. They have asked us to be sure that things are in good shape when we leave. We would appreciate anything any of you who have an extra minute could do to help us get the room together."

They reorganized chairs, put on a fresh pot of coffee, cleaned the blackboard, and did everything that needed to be done. We were still talking with participants, and they even moved us around to get everything in perfect order.

By inviting their contribution and encouraging them to assist, we received extra effort. But by demanding specifically through a directive, this lady received resistance and hostility.

TWO QUESTIONS

There are two questions we may ask ourselves whenever we are about to *direct* another human being.

1. "Will the world come to a screeching, irrevocable halt if I don't handle every detail of this transaction my way?"

That may sound humorous, but what we are really asking is if there are really major life-threatening, critical things that could go wrong if we allow this person a moment of dignity in this transaction. If there are, then we should step in and handle it. However, directing should be our last, considered response, not our first knee-jerk reaction.

If the answer to the first question is, "No," then we can ask the second question.

2. Is their any possibility that this human being will ever have to develop plans of his or her own during his or her lifetime?"

If the answer is, "Yes," then we should avoid directing. How do people learn to develop plans of their own if they are never encouraged to plan something? How do they ever learn to confront holes in their plans if they are never allowed the dignity of a plan with a hole in it, or they are made to feel so dumb for the hole that they are afraid to try again?

The greatest successes in life frequently come from failures we designed ourselves from which we gained understanding but didn't take so personally that we were afraid to try.

BUILDER NO. 3 — ENCOURAGING/INVITING

In the above examples we see that whenever people are invited or encouraged to contribute, they generally are more willing, cooperative, and responsive. When my *neighbor* says, "I have company coming soon and would appreciate it if you would straighten up the family room," the same kids that left the socks usually do a pretty thorough job because they were respected.

We are encouraging to children when we *see them as assets* rather than objects, when we *see mistakes as opportunities* to learn rather than as failures, and when we *invite participation and contribution* rather than directing and demanding compliance.

Jonas Salk understood the concept of being encouraging. He was once asked, "How does this outstanding experiment, which has effectively brought an end to the word polio in our vocabulary, cause you to look back on your previous 200 failures?"

His response (paraphrased) was, "I never had 200 failures in my life. My family didn't think in terms of failure. They taught in terms of experiences and what could be learned. I just made my 201st discovery. I couldn't have made it without learning from the previous 200 experiences."

Winston Churchill was raised that way. He was not intimidated by an error. He just thought it through and did better. Someone once said to him, "Sir Winston, what in your school experience best prepared you to lead Britain out of her darkest hour?"

Winston thought a minute and then said, "It was the two years I spent at the same level in high school."

"Did you fail?"

"No," replied Winston, "I had two opportunities to get it

73

right. What Britain needed was not brilliance, but perseverance when things were going badly."

We help young people develop positive attitudes of learning from experience and not being discouraged by seeming failures when we are encouraging and invite them to explore possibilities.

Mr. Hanson asked his child what he needed to have ready for his field trip on the weekend. He listened and heard some holes in the plan but none that could hurt his child seriously.

When he got back from the field trip, Mr. Hanson asked him how it went. He said, "Not so great. I was hungry and cold."

He asked, "Why?"

The child said, "I didn't have much food or a jacket. I forgot to check the weather, and I didn't plan for enough food."

Mr. Hanson asked, "What would you do differently next time now that you have had this experience?"

"Well, I think I will check the weather, and prepare for three meals a day."

The first step of this process was the encouragement of asking what was needed to be ready for the field trip. The teaching part incorporates returning to Builder No. 2 (Exploring) when he gets home after having the experience. *Directing* would have occurred if this parent had stepped in and told him all the things he should have ready for his trip. By *inviting* and *encouraging* him to plan, this parent avoided the *barrier of directing* him in what to do. Then when the child arrived home, the parent used the *builder of exploring* rather than the *barrier of explaining*, to confirm the value of the experience in his mind.

One sets up the other. By having been patient in the first place, this father set up a climate for teaching.

I had a foster son who had a similar experience. After he came home from a trip, I asked, "What did you learn during the trip?"

He replied, "I was reminded about how much I hate bologna."

I asked, "What do you mean?"

He said, "That was all people were willing to loan me."

I said, "Well from that, what do you plan to do on your next trip?"

He said, "I'm going to take a bucket of chicken for me and some bologna for the suckers who forget."

BARRIER NO. 4 — EXPECTING

Expecting is the art of setting high standards and then pointing out children's failure to reach these standards, an attitude which always discourages and destroys them.

Should we have high expectations for our children? There is some debate on this because we don't know how to make our expectations encouraging.

William Glasser said, "Children find in the eyes of their parents, the mirrors in which they define themselves in the relationship. Fill them with nothing, they become nothing. They have a tremendous ability to live down to the lowest expectation in any environment."

We should have the highest possible expectation for those we love but not engage in *expecting*. *High expectations* represent a belief in the capabilities of children which is followed by effective methods of helping them develop and grow toward their potential. *Expecting* represents a disbelief in their capabilities which is followed by criticism of their failures.

Every religion which preaches perfection as a standard and then endlessly points out where people are failing to reach it will have a large, depressed, dropped out, vulnerable, unreconcilable constituency. However, the churches that set perfection as a goal and then are quick to celebrate any apparent movement toward it have an inspired, growing, excited group of people.

We should have high expectations, but anticipate that children will move toward them in little steps and small increments.

If we don't have high expectations of our children, then they won't have a clear vision of their capabilities. But if we then engage in *expecting* and constantly point out where our children fall short, we will reduce their perceptions of their capabilities.

I expect my child to learn to make his bed, but I anticipate he will learn to do it in little steps. So we start out with something he can do. He can straighten his cover. He can fluff up his pillow. Over time he will develop better skills.

We can have high expectations, but be quick to celebrate as they move closer: "You got your cover and pillow straightened up today, and that is an important part of getting your bed made."

To expect perfection in the beginning is unreasonable, but to expect that the child will become capable of doing an excellent job in small steps is reasonable.

BUILDER NO. 4 — CELEBRATING

It is an interesting to watch how children respond. When we are quick to celebrate any little movement in the right direction, we seem to get more movement.

Celebrating is recognizing progress, "Son, I appreciate the fact that the cupboard was straightened up and that the dishes were put in the sink." No "buts."

We are often fixated on "buts." Whenever a compliment is given, we wait for the "but." "Nice job on this and this, but _____." That destroys the value of the compliment and increases sensitivity to criticism since the child suspects there will usually be a "but."

Adults are often preoccupied with what is not happening in the relationship and overlook what is happening. How many times have we seen a parent come home, ignore that the cupboard was cleaned up and the dishes were in the sink, and comment only on the fact that the trash wasn't taken out. When we focus on the negative and ignore the positive, we make children feel, "It is better not to waste any time and effort doing things because they won't notice anyway. All they notice is what I didn't do."

Soon a child will say, "If I just ignore this parent all together and do nothing, she will run around doing it herself while she is yelling at me. All I have to perfect is my ability to ignore the yelling, and I'm home free."

It is easier to tame a fanatic than to put life into a corpse. When we set high expectations and then point out people's deficiencies, we discourage them and create corpses that we have to endlessly pump up and carry along.

When we are quick to *celebrate* any little movement in the right direction, then we affirm and validate people and often get people fanatically interested in doing more.

If we raise children to be independent, self-reliant people, they *will be*. Sometimes we put young people in a double bind because we try to help them become independent and then get upset when they are independent in ways of their own choosing.

Garrison Keillor tells the following story in his book, *Lake Wobegon Days*, which illustrates these concepts:

Our Sunday School class learned *Joy to the World* for the Christmas Program. You asked me to sing it for the Aunts and Uncles when they came to dinner. I said, "No, please."

You said, "Yes, please."

I said, "No."

You said, "Someday when I'm dead and in my coffin, maybe

you'll look down and remember the times I asked you to do things and you wouldn't."

So I sang, terrified of them, and terrified about your death, and you stopped me halfway through; you said, "Now, come on, you can sing better than that."

A few years later when I sang the part of Curly in *Oklahoma!* and everybody else said it was wonderful.

You said, "I told him for years he could sing, and he wouldn't listen to me."

But I did listen to you and that's most of my problem. Everything you said went in one ear and down my spine. Now you call me on the phone to ask, "Why don't you ever call us? Why do you shut us out of your life?"

So I start to tell you about my life. But you don't want to hear it. You want to know why I didn't call. I didn't call because I don't need to talk to you anymore. You voice is in my head, talking constantly from morning until night. I keep my radio turned on, but I still hear you, and I will hear you all my life, until the day I die, when I will hear you say, "I told you."

THE DOUBLE BIND

My father was put in this double bind. His mother had said to him as a child, "You can't go swimming until you learn how to swim because you might drown."

His whole life he could never let go enough to learn to swim for fear he would drown. The first time he ever leaned forward and trusted himself to the water was when a group of grandchildren contrived to outfit him in swim flugels at every joint, wrapped him in several water ski belts and flotation jackets, and let him hold a float while they pushed him into deep water. They filmed the whole event. It took 53 years and innovative grandchildren to overcome the double bind of expectations that his mother had put him in.

Timing is important when improvement is needed. Celebration of improvement should stand alone. At a later time we can say, "Honey, these dishes are getting in the way for me now. I would appreciate it if you would come in here and get them out of the way for me now." Needed improvement can be dealt with as a separate transaction.

Then children feel, "Boy, even if I don't get everything together, they notice and appreciate what I did do, so it is worth trying."

We would like to separate expectations from anticipations.

77

Children can understand, "I expect you will become all you can, and I anticipate that you will meet my expectations in a series of small steps within your reach. Therefore, any time you take a small step, you have fulfilled my anticipations and have moved toward your potential. That is a reason for great joy."

A child who has never tried to wash clothes before, who one day takes the initiative and runs the washer with only a sweat shirt in it, should not be criticized for wasting water and soap.

Celebrate what went right. Later, when it happens again, begin to leave a few more clothes in a basket by the washer and suggest including them.

I have seen many boys taken to the golf course and intimidated into hating golf by a father who wanted excellence the first day instead of letting the boy enjoy going along and trying a little at a time.

When we celebrate any movement in the right direction, then we are saying that we anticipate that the movement will occur in sometimes very tiny increments. We can then be alert for them and joyful when they occur. With this attitude we tend to inspire everyone around us.

Studies of successful, healthy people show that they are consistent *good finders* who see lemonade in lemons and the glass that is half full rather than half empty.

Incidently, people who are quick to celebrate any little movement in the right direction have very few problems with burnout and stress. People who look at what has not been done or what they did not accomplish during the day, who go to bed and burn themselves out in stress, tend to invalidate themselves and others. We need to be fair with ourselves also and celebrate and concentrate on any good that we accomplish, so that when we go to sleep we will become refreshed and renewed during the night. We will then be ready for our best effort the next day.

BARRIER NO. 5 — ADULTISMS

One of the single most destructive behaviors that we find in relationships, and probably the thing that does the most damage, is what we call *isming*. So many negative things in our culture get an *ism*. We tend to put *isms* on things that are problems, painful, and/or sicknesses such as alcoholism, workaholism, and recidivism when we relapse after improvement. *Isming*, in this book, refers to a process in relationships of requiring other people to read our mind and to think as we do.

Spousism occurs when one spouse requires another spouse to think, understand, see, and do things exactly as he or she does. "You knew what I wanted." "You should have known." "If you really cared, I wouldn't have to tell you."

Supervisorism occurs when a supervisor holds us accountable for having all of his or her knowledge and for understanding just what he or she understands about everything: "Surely you realize." "You knew what we were expecting."

Teacherism occurs in the classroom when a person with a master's degree or doctorate in a subject assumes that an eight- year-old should have the same comprehension he or she has of an issue or idea and asks, "Why is this important?"

An *adultism* occurs any time an adult forgets what it is like to be a child and then expects, demands, and requires of the child, who has never been an adult, to think, act, understand, see, and do things as an adult. These unrealistic expectations from adults produce impotence, frustration, hostility and aggression in young people. It undercuts the value of expressions of love. It destroys their belief in their capabilities, their significance, and their influence over events; yet, we imply these expectations many times a day.

The language of adultism is, "Why can't you ever? How come you never? Surely you realize! How many times do I have to tell you? Why are you so childish? When will you ever grow up? Did you? Can you? Will you? Won't you?" Are you? Aren't you?"

It begins like this: "Why can't you clean up your room?" This adult has forgotten what it was like to be a child. I remember my room when I was a child? To my mother, it was the center of her Universe. To me, it was only a pitstop on my way to immortality. From that perspective, look what we did to each other.

She would say, "Clean your room."

I would say, "I did," meaning I have passed through it twice without tripping.

She would say, "No, you didn't," meaning she could not eat off the floor. "What will the neighbors think?"

Now that I have married, some twenty years later, I have discovered that my wife, like my mother, honestly believes that the neighbors come by every night to peer in the window. If by chance they don't come by to check us out in terms of how clean our bedrooms are, then her mother comes by on her broom or her cloud, however you figure she is traveling these days. Either way, we spend our whole lives trying to live up to other people's expectations.

Now I have bought one of these bedrooms. I have furnished it, put in an FM radio and an electric blanket. I hope to hang out there a few times a week unmolested. It has become the center of my Universe. Now I can't understand why kids want to use bedrooms for pitstops.

Can you imagine how disillusioning it is? My firstborn child arrived 19 years ago on the planet. We thought she was average and were desperate to prove it. We weaned her on schedule, potty trained her on schedule, and forced her off to school two years before we were ready. We did everything right and relaxed. That is where we blew it, I think.

A short time ago, nature began to deliver. Her body began to develop. She began to flip her hair and the neighbors out all at the same time and totally lost her perspective. Now, in spite of several years of hassling, if you gave her a choice at this very moment between standing out on our lawn talking with a 19-year-old hunk in a Firebird or being in her closet stacking her shoes on those racks we bought for her, she chooses the hunk in the Firebird every time. We have no idea what is causing it. We are having her tested for emotional retardation and learning disabilities. We have tried every way to encourage her. We say, "How can you live like this? What kind of a pig would do that? Recently I thought of this one, "If you ever get a husband, he will leave in a day when he sees your room." But, it is as if she has a mental block. Some essential cog has slipped in her intellectual repertoire.

What has really slipped is my understanding that people see things differently, based upon the priorities of their life at the moment.

Adolescence is a time for discovering yourself. It is a very important time where much of the focus is *inside*. Building friends is so much more important than having a tidy bedroom. Finding an identity, discovering oneself, sorting through feelings is infinitely more critical than getting laundry done right after school. Adolescence is a poor time to demand thoughtfulness, consideration, and insight about important issues and events.

If we demand more with, "Why can't you ever? How come you never? Surely you realize. You'll never learn. Why can't you be thoughtful?" we have just pounded a lot of unnecessary nails of discouragement and we soon get a child who believes that questions are things adults use to get kids to expose themselves so adults can kill them. They learn that the best possible response to anything we ask is, "I don't know."

"I don't know" is a great defensive tactic for young people who have heard too many adultisms.

An *ism* is destructive because it requires mind reading and makes everyone who doesn't think, see, and understand exactly like us, feel less than acceptable to us. *Isms* ignore the uniqueness of perception and is overtly non-supportive.

BUILDER NO. 5 — RESPECT

The language of *respect* is, "What was your understanding of _____? Let me be sure I understand? Under what circumstances would you need to check with me?"

It is very easy to slip into *threatening, correcting, directing*, and *expecting* when we are very busy, with very little time and lots to do. Soon we can *threaten, correct, direct*, and *expect* ourselves right into bedtime. In the process we lose the affirmation and validation which can be experienced through dialogue.

When we can substitute *respect* for those *adultisms*, and understand that attitudes and behaviors come from perceptions and beliefs, instead of confronting the behavior, we will explore the beliefs. Young people can not gain wisdom as long as they are afraid to have the experience or if we spend all the time analyzing it for them so they never get the chance to master wisdom from their experiences. If we insist that we have more knowledge than young people have had a chance to accumulate, they will be intimidated by the process of gathering knowledge. If we *expect* them to see what we see instead of *exploring* what they see and then comparing notes, we have wiped them out. And, anytime we demand automatically with, "Why can't you ever. How come you never," we create threat. Threat that young people will let us down again. Threat that they will prove inadequate if they open their mouths.

So, how are we going to affect their perceptions if support must precede a challenge? We can not challenge perceptions effectively if we attack them first?

We have to respect all five dimensions of perception to avoid the adultisms. The language of respect is, "What was your understanding of what I needed done in the family room? What is your understanding of what I need to have you do to have this bedroom straightened up? What plans do you have for having this mess cleared up by the time your father gets home?"

To the spouse, "What was your understanding of what I planned to take with me on this trip?"

In the classroom, "What ideas did you get from this paragraph as you read it? In addition to that, how many of you became aware of this, and what is your understanding of that as I have been explaining it to you?"

It is also important that we recognize that on the job, "You knew what we wanted on that project," is far less affirming than, "What was your understanding of what we needed to have done on that project?"

To say, "Honey, where are my brown pants? You knew I would need them from the cleaners. Every week it is the same thing. Nothing is ever ready," is infinitely less affirming than, "Honey, what was your understanding of what I was planning to take with me on this trip?"

In the classroom, "What do we mean by this sentence," instead of, "What things did you get out of this sentence that could be meaningful?" One invites thinking and contributing. One invites self-defense and passivity. It is our choice.

Once we use, "What? Where? When? How? In what way? under what circumstances?" we have shown respect for the uniqueness of perception.

And so, we must make room for individual perception with great respect or we deny the greatest beauty of the human race, our diversity. We must stop picking people apart for being different and celebrate the strength that is in that diversity. It is in our very uniqueness that we have our greatest value to each other.

WE DON'T HAVE TO BE PERFECT

Do you see one of the above barriers that you regularly create with someone you love? Do you believe that, if you worked at it, you could do them less often? We are not suggesting you must never do any of them. My children endure adultisms 20% of the time, but they will say, "The majority of the time Dad deals with us firmly, but with dignity and respect, so he must be having a bad day. Check him out tomorrow."

If they heard adultisms most of the time, they would be more likely to say, "Don't fool with Dad on any terms. Most days are likely to be bad with him. Get high, get loaded, get stoned, get out of there, but don't get in his way."

PUTTING THEM ALL TOGETHER

Suppose four-year-old Linda becomes stuck when her tricycle wheel runs off the sidewalk. A parent could handle this situation in several ways that would decrease feelings of capability:

Directing : "Don't just sit there and cry. Get off and push the tricycle back on the sidewalk."

82

Directing children through each step instead of exploring how a task could be accomplished sends the message that they are not capable enough to do the task on their own without specific directions.

Explaining : "That is what happens when you don't watch where you are going."

Explaining what happened and how to fix it, instead of helping children examine and analyze their own problems, is neglecting an opportunity to give children the perception that they are capable.

Rescuing : "Don't cry, honey. I will fix it for you."

If we rush in and *save* our children, we are directly telling them that they are incapable of taking care of their life. By allowing them to take the consequences of their actions, we are telling them they are capable of handling their own behavior and the consequences.

Assuming : "Be sure that you don't let your wheel come off the edge of the sidewalk, because your bike will get stuck."

This example shows a combination of barriers. Assuming that the child would not stay away from the edge of the sidewalk led to directing. The directing included trying to *rescue* the child in advance. Assuming keeps us from letting the child have a chance to ride down the sidewalk and discover the problem for herself. Using these barriers can create an extremely frustrating experience for children.

Adultisms : "You knew you were supposed to keep the handlebars straight. How come you never keep your eyes on the sidewalk? Why can't you ever do it right? Surely you realize what will happen if you don't! When will you ever listen?"

Children feel personally attacked by adultisms because the implication is, "Well I should have known you are not big enough to ride a tricycle by yourself yet."

By attacking *the person* and not pointing to *the problem*, adults make children feel worthless and incapable.

What then?

"Whoops! Honey, what do you think would happen if you got off your tricycle and backed it up?

That question may seem very similar to explaining or directing, but there is a very subtle and important difference. The final answer must come from Linda after she pauses to consider the question and perhaps even tries it to find out what would happen.

ATTITUDE

The key component in all of the barriers and builders is attitude. The attitudes inherent in the barriers are negative and disrespectful. The attitudes inherent in the builders are positive and respectful.

It could be nothing more than an our tone of voice that invites children to consider their own capabilities. Our tone of voice changes when we change out attitudes.

Scott enjoyed being with his friends more than he enjoyed being home. When he did come home, his mother would say in a sarcastic tone of voice, "Well, it's about time you came home." This remark only confirmed Scott's decision that home was not a pleasant place to be.

When Scott's mother changed her attitude, Scott enjoyed being home more often. The next time Scott came home late she said, "I'm so glad to see you. I really enjoy having you around." The results were positive because of the respectful atmosphere created by the change in attitude.

BARRIERS DEFEAT — BUILDERS WIN

One father shared that his family had been through two treatment programs, three psychiatrists, and two psychologists. They had given up hope of any kind of relationship with their daughter. "Within a week of learning about the *barriers* and *builders*, we experienced a level of closeness, trust, and communication that I personally would have said was not possible with that daughter. But I discovered that I was doing all five of the five of barriers daily. As soon as I cut down the frequency of the barriers, even before I learned to use the builders, her responsiveness increased dramatically."

The *barriers* teach children to be passive and unresponsive. When we command, "Pick that up. Put that away. It is time to get in here and get something to eat," we will soon have children who are very resistant.

The *builders* not only build perceptions of capability, significance and influence, but when we remove the *five barriers*, we create a climate of respect in which dialogue is likely to occur.

The next step in helping children develop strong perceptions of personal capabilities is to structure situations where they can recognize and understand appropriate behaviors and role models.

CHILDREN SEE, CHILDREN DO

Children sharpen their self-evaluation skills when we dialogue with them about what they admire in people. We can model for them by being articulate and specific in stating things we admire.

We can follow up with the EIAG. "What was it you admired in that person? In what way is that an admirable thing for you? How could you show that same kind of characteristic in your life?"

If young people have never identified the capabilities they admire, then how do they internalize them? It is the young people without a sense of their own capabilities who imitate others.

Chimpanzees and gorillas copy each other, but human beings, if encouraged to do so, can look at people they encounter and thoughtfully decide what they do or do not want to copy. It is particularly good for adolescents to read fiction and talk about the things the characters did or the things they believed and stood for. They can be specific in discussing things about the characters that they admired or that they did not admire.

The Japanese endlessly study the lives of successful people, not to copy them, but to learn the principles that made them successful so they can fit these principles into their own lives.

It is very important that young people, rather than imitate the hero, learn to respect what is heroic about the hero because tomorrow the hero may be seen as drug addicted, criminal, or imperfect in some other way in addition to what he or she did well.

THE INFLUENCE OF MEDIA MODELS

The media has a tremendous impact on children today. They spend an average of 18,000 hours watching television from birth to 18 years of age. During that time they see an average of 180,000 minutes of commercials teaching them self-medication and instant gratification, that warmth and closeness are easily obtainable when we use the right product or services and that sports heroes and other celebrities gain success through hustling beverages and products.

Since these are the heroes and influences that are so prevalent in society today, we need to compensate by helping children think critically about what they see and observe and by modeling the things we value in our relationship with them.

When we *assume, rescue, direct, expect*, and use *adultisms* we are modeling a lack of belief in the capabilities of children. They react by being defensive, distant, and unresponsive.

"Do as I say, not as I do," does not inspire trust and admiration in children. They will more likely do as you do, or go to the other extreme, and do the opposite of what you do.

This does not mean that your children cannot learn what you have not learned, nor that they cannot do what you have not been able to do. Many parents have felt defeated because they mistakenly believed they could not teach their children what they could not do themselves.

It is very important to inspire this generation of young people who must go into a world where new discoveries are being made at a faster rate than ever before. Those who are equipped to learn how to create their own way will be the most successful.

The highest accolade that a parent or teacher can ever be given is that their children and their students became more capable than they were.

Chapter 5

HELPING CHILDREN FEEL MEANING, PURPOSE, AND SIGNIFICANCE

The second of the *significant seven* approaches the core of human existence and the greatest human need. The greatest human need is to find meaning, purpose, and status in life — and to perceive and experience personal significance.

THE NEED TO BE NEEDED

The need to be needed is often more powerful than the need to survive. Human beings are the only species who sometimes commit suicide due to their perception of not having meaning, purpose, and significance to their life.

Alfred Adler found that when human beings do not feel *belonging and significance* they find *mistaken* ways of behaving to achieve a pseudo sense of significance. Some of the *mistaken* behaviors are to seek significance through demanding undue attention, using power in unproductive ways, seeking revenge for perceived, or to simply *give up*.

When human beings believe they are insignificant and unnecessary, they may respond with active, rebellious behavior or in passive resignation. Rebellion often takes the form of drug and alcohol abuse, vandalism, and teenage pregnancy. Resignation often takes the form of anorexia, suicide, an overt lack of the will to live, depression, illness, premature senility and death. These are all correlated with a lack of perception of meaning and purpose in life.

Studies have shown that babies and children placed in orphanages where they are supervised in groups and everything is done for them show developmental retardation, health problems, and even death in above normal frequencies.

Children placed in virtually identical settings with staff trained to

1. Spend individual time each day with each child

2. Practice dialogue with each child

3. Organize significant tasks and activities in ways that invite assistance from individual children show accelerated development, lower than normal frequencies of health problems, and death.

Recent studies into the chemistry of the brain show that many of the critical brain chemicals that regulate mood, motivation, concentration, feelings, resistance to illness, and depression are highly influenced by perceptions of personal significance.

THE NEED IS FOREVER

Young people are not the only ones who suffer from the lack of meaning, purpose, and significance that comes from being needed. At the other end of the spectrum, problems are similar for older people. Modern medical technology and improved diet have increased the average life expectancy by 30 years. So we increased the life span at the same time we eliminated the role of older people in community networks. They no longer have any role in the parenting process or on-the-job training for the next generation. Those were critical roles for older people prior to World War II. As a result, many older people experience depression, disillusionment, despair, premature senility, and even death from that lack of affirmation.

Some research has shown that older people who have a pet or a plant that they believe needs them will live several years longer than people without a pet or a plant. Very frequently, when the pet or plant dies, so do the older people who own them. Paul Harvey told the following story: An eighty-year-old man was cutting down trees on his farm with his chainsaw so he and his wife would have firewood for the winter. As he was cutting through one of the trees, it bucked off the stump, came down on his foot, and crushed it. As the tree fell over, it drove the chainsaw through three fingers of his hand and then into his esophagus and trachea. As the chainsaw was cutting through his throat, he had a vision of his wife who was ill. He knew there was no one who was aware of her or who would take care of her, and that she would be left alone in the farmhouse. He became so concerned for her that he pulled the chainsaw from his body, threw the tree off his foot, and hobbled half a mile on what was left of his body. He stayed alive because of the overwhelming power of the belief that he was genuinely and uniquely needed by someone.

BEING NEEDED IS EMPOWERING

In previous generations, doctors, nurses, and clergy went through incredible epidemics, violated every rule of contagion, worked to the point of exhaustion, and still did not usually contract the illness because of the incredible power of their belief that only they were left to do what needed to be done for others.

Recent research in the field of medicine has shown that a specific perception of significance, uniqueness, and being needed on a job or by a family has a significant affect in reducing the risk to cancer, strokes, heart attack, hypertension, and other diseases. This perception also increases the probability of recovering. So even at the most basic level of our resistance to illness and disease and our motivation to live comes the direct need to believe that we play a contributing role in the lives of people who matter to us.

COMPENSATIONS

In Chapter Two we discussed the loss of meaningful roles for young people in our culture and suggested some possible alternatives. In a world where we really don't need children in practical ways, the process of developing perceptions of significance is greatly complicated. This is why the *barrier* behaviors discussed in the last chapter are doubly powerful today since they also reduce perceptions of personal significance.

Using the *builders*, on the other hand, enhances perceptions of personal significance. When adults *direct* young people, they make everything a *chore*. When adults invite the assistance of young people, they are given a chance to *contribute*.

Young people who have many chores may feel insignificant and frustrated as did Cinderella in the classic fairy tale. People are affirmed when they believe that who they are and what they are doing is valued by people as a contribution, not a chore. When the prince decided that his life would not be the same without the unique contribution of Cinderella, she threw off the yoke of depression and despair and began to look at life differently.

Today, more than ever, rituals, traditions, and collaboration within family systems are at a premium since they are scarce. Whenever possible we are well advised to invite the contributions of others and practice the art of affirmation.

ACTIVITIES THAT DEVELOP A SENSE OF MEANING AND PURPOSE

Significant adults can guide young people into activities that develop that sense of meaning and purpose. We now find that when we have *cross-age tutoring* in which older young people teach younger people, the tutors do better than the tutorees because they are needed. When we have *peer counseling*, the counselors do better than the counselees because they are needed. We find that even delinquent young people, when recruited into programs to work with and *do things for younger people*, tend to resolve much of their delinquent behavior under the affirmation of being needed and being significant.

Affirmation is very critical. Alcoholics Anonymous and many other groups have shown that when people are needed as a contributor, they bond, invest, grow, and get healthy. When everything is done for them, they remain inadequate and insignificant. Over and over we find that it is only when the *helpee* becomes the *helper* that he or she gains dignity and self-respect.

When we do too much for our children, we put them in the position of the *helpee* and rob them of meaningful roles which give them the position of the *helper* with the inherent opportunities to maintain their dignity and self-respect. Involving children in family rituals and traditions is an excellent way to provide practice in meaningful roles and the opportunity to feel significant through meaningful contribution.

FAMILY RITUALS AND TRADITIONS

Children develop perceptions of meaning, purpose, relevance, and significance when they have an opportunity to participate in *meaningful* family rituals and traditions on a regular basis.

A friend once said, "Why is it today that we will keep every important business appointment except the one with the group we're in the most important business with?"

Families once did almost everything together. They had to plant, harvest, store, build, and do all the other essential tasks for survival. They needed each other.

Today families are often going in so many different directions they hardly see each other. When they are in the same house they are often hassling over things that *should* be done, but don't

have to be done; or they may be watching television instead of interacting together.

Research from many sources has made it clear that the
stronger a child's perceptions of being an important, contributing
part of a functioning set of relationships on any on-going basis before
the age of twelve, the more resistant he or she will be to peer groups,
cults, and programming generally in their teenage years.

Families that devote any regular time — as little as 30 minutes a week with small children or 30 minutes a month with older
children — to some regularly structured ritual, tradition, or activity,
have a much lower incidence of children in serious difficulty than
identical families in the same neighborhoods that don't spend time
together.

Since we do not *have* to do things together for our survival,
it is important that we structure meaningful activities to build close
relationships. We need to create a climate of support where we can
help young people develop the important perceptions and skills they
need for successful living.

Family meetings are an extremely effective ritual and tradition and can be the process used for family involvement in deciding
on other rituals and traditions that will be meaningful for each family.

FAMILY MEETINGS

Participation in the family meeting process meets many
needs which help children develop strong perceptions of meaning,
purpose, and significance:

1. Effective dialogue is essential to successful family meetings,
   and this process provides a time and place to practice dialogue.

2. Family meetings become an important ritual and tradition
   when family members know they can count on having meetings take place on a regular basis, preferably at least once a
   week. Many families take the phone of the hook during their
   family meetings and ask friends not to call during that time.

3. Beginning family meetings with compliments or acknowledge-
   ments is an excellent way for family members to learn the skill
   of looking for nice things to acknowledge about each other
   and to learn the skill of being able to verbalize positive feed-

back. Too often we are more comfortable giving and receiving negative criticism than we are with commendations.

4. Young people have an opportunity to feel significant when the chairperson position is rotated. The chairperson calls the meeting to order, calls on people who want to speak, and generally follows parliamentary procedure.

Other benefits and procedures for family meetings will be discussed in the next chapter.

SPIRITUAL AFFIRMATION

Many, including the authors, believe that human beings are basically spiritual creatures. If we define spirituality as an active sense of identification with things greater than one's self which gives life meaning and purpose, then many things religious are not spiritual, and many things spiritual are not religious. Friendship, trust, loyalty, affirmation, and respect are all inherently spiritual.

THREE CONDITIONS NECESSARY TO MEET THIS NEED

Three conditions are necessary for people to experience meaning, purpose, and significance in life which provide the core of spiritual affirmation.

1. To be listened to — not just heard, but understood.

2. To be taken seriously, — not just understood, but accepted and given unconditional love, care, and respect.

3. To be genuinely needed — affirmed for personal worth, contributions, and significance.

John Naisbett, in his best selling book, *Megatrends*, raised the issue of *high tech* versus *high touch*, indicating that as our lifestyle became saturated with *high tech*, we began to experience deficits in what he called *high touch*, or personal contact and affirmation. He went on to explore the role of *quality circles* and other vehicles used in a business setting to help people feel listened to, taken seriously, and significant. As we immersed ourselves in *high tech*, we began to preempt the dialogue and collaboration that kept us in touch with each other, and most relationship systems became more stressful.

THE ART OF AFFIRMATION

We believe that *high touch* refers to the art of affirmation. The basic needs referred to in this chapter — to be listened to, taken seriously, and affirmed in one's significance — constitute the concept of *high touch* or validation.

The second of the *significant seven* is to develop a sense of personal significance in people. Therefore, the art of affirmation involves learning to help young people feel listened to, taken seriously, and significant in what we do with them.

DIALOGUE

Dialogue is surfacing in many places in the research as being the foundation of critical thinking, moral and ethical development, judgmental maturity, bonding, closeness, and trust. Dialogue is defined as a meaningful exchange of perceptions in a non-threatening climate of support and genuine interest. It is almost impossible in our society for young people to feel meaning, purpose, and significance without engaging in meaningful dialogue with significant others.

GENUINE INTEREST

Dialogue through the EIAG process should only be used to genuinely explore a person's perceptions and to genuinely encourage them to discover new perceptions about a situation. To accomplish this, our attitude has to be one of respect and genuine interest.

Our attitude will show through, even when we are not aware of it. A mother who was working on her attitude decided she was going to convey to her son that he was a priority to her. She saw lots of ways in which she had not been doing this. When he came into the room to talk with her, she reached over and turned the radio off. Her son stopped talking, looked at her in amazement, and said, "Why did you do that?"

She answered, "Well, I just wanted to hear what you had to say."

He retorted, "Well, is that something that you learned in your workshop?"

She said, "Well, as a matter of fact I did. I learned that if you were important to me, I would take the steps to pay full attention to what you said."

He said, "Well, you don't need to do that."

She was a little concerned that maybe it wasn't working. It was explained to her that most human beings are a little embarrassed when they receive unexpected attention. When asked how he responded, she said, "He went ahead and told me what he was going to say, and he beamed a little bit."

I queried her some more, "Even though he told you that you didn't have to do that, did he go back and turn the radio on?"

She said, "No."

"Did he go ahead and share with you?"

She said, "Yes."

"Did you hear him a little more clearly?"

She said, "Yes."

"Did you achieve your goal of showing him that he was significant?"

She said, "Yes."

If this mother's attempts seem sudden and awkward, the story illustrates that the key to the successful application of these principles is attitude. Our attitudes are determined by what we believe about people and *how* we ask the EIAG questions. They can be an interrogation and produce resistance. Sometimes they can be manipulative, when we want to prove a point we have already decided.

It could be that this mother had changed her attitude but her son was not ready to perceive a difference.

The most important factor leading to the success or failure of the EIAG process is perceptions. Even when our attitude is one of respect and genuine interest, it is possible that our children will not perceive it that way.

It may especially be difficult for children to get used to changes in our attitudes. They may continue to react based on our former behavior. It may take time and patience to allow for a shift in perceptions.

Adolescents, and most of us, are sometimes embarrassed when trying to deal with needs and feelings. We may feel confused and respond awkwardly.

We can't go necessarily by what people say. Adolescents may feel confused by needing our affirmation at the same time they are trying to show their independence. They are encouraged by our concern and interest and discouraged when we press them and try to force them to open up all the way on our terms.

How would you respond to, "Why can't you ever? How come you never? Surely you realize? How many times must I tell you?" You could very quickly become as wise as a child and say, "I don't know."

"I DON'T KNOW," IS SAFE

Do you know why kids say, "I don't know?" Usually it is because they learn very early in life that questions are things that adults use to get kids to expose themselves so adults can attack them. They learn the safest response to any adult question is, "I don't know."

Many of the changes that we have identified in previous chapters have worked against dialogue. The loss of time, the loss of a structure, the changes in school, and very frequently being called upon to repeat back someone else's ideas rather than to have a safe place to explore one's own thoughts and ideas all create fundamental barriers to the process of dialogue. To the extent that the dialogue process is compromised in a relationship, it will a less affirming and less validating. This lack of affirming and validating relationships with significant adults creates a less supportive climate for young people to grow, change, and learn.

The *baby boom*, our response to it, and our subsequent preoccupation with what we might call more content oriented rote and recall models of education, have also undercut dialogue. Many people call this approach to learning Skinnerian learning, although B. F. Skinner moved steadily over his career to a more perceptually and transactionally based model for working with human beings.

In 1986 the National Assessment Project, established by the U. S. Congress to monitor America's school improvement effort, presented data to the National Association of Secondary School Administrators indicating that American children were not showing significant changes in the areas of critical thinking, judgmental maturity, and the emergence of moral and ethical capabilities after they leave the sixth grade.

Whatever they have developed by the sixth grade is generally what they have in the twelfth grade. Although they were prepared to go well beyond this level in terms of their developmental potential, they were obviously not taking the necessary steps. Researchers traced much of this retarded development to the overuse of objective tests at the secondary level. Objective tests are easier to grade and to handle; however, the needs of the students is for more interaction, more dialogue, more collaboration with their teachers, more case studies, more essay exams, and more dialogue and challenge.

They also found that a strong tendency for secondary teachers to grade or correct grammar, but not engage in any significant dialogue about the organization, implications, alternatives, thoughts, ideas, and structure of the student's paper, was working directly against the developmental needs of this age group.

As children pass the age of eight developmentally, they move into a zone in which they begin to substitute thought, volition, insight, and understanding for rote and recall. But to take this jump and become what Kolberg called a conventional human being in their reasoning, they have to have dialogue and collaborative experiences with more mature people. Our culture has moved directly away from providing opportunities for dialogue and collaboration with young people.

Young people (and many adults) are afraid to think and explore when they have been taught that they will be penalized if they say the wrong thing. Those who really want to encourage children to think and explore are being blocked in their efforts by the awareness of children at the age of six or seven that it is not safe to offer what you think, but to guess what the teacher wants.

One teacher who attended a leadership training workshop said, "For the last nineteen years as a teacher, I have been rendering children impotent in my classroom with my teaching methods and then criticizing them for their lack of initiative. But the chickens came home to roost last night:

My daughter came home with several questions on her math homework. One of the questions was, 'Which of the following charts do you like best and why?' The next questions was, 'Which of the following charts do you like least and why?' The third question was, 'Which did you find easiest to understand and why?' My daughter was desperate because she had not compared notes with the other kids to find out which one the teacher wanted them to pick. I discussed with her that these were questions inviting her to make her own choice and justify it. She said, 'You don't understand this teacher. If I pick the one she doesn't want, I will suffer. My grade is marginal, and I need to do well.' I argued with her for awhile. She finally grudgingly took out a sheet of paper and answered the questions as she saw them. In the morning I found that paper in the trash. She was off early to talk with the other kids to try to guess which answers the teacher wanted."

This child had learned that one of the riskiest things of all is to insert a personal opinion. It was far easier to give the teacher what she wanted than to take the risk of thinking.

ADULTISMS VS. UNDERSTANDING

We have a whole culture attending workshops on family stress, intimacy, communication, and parenting skills, who then go home and paint themselves in a corner with, "Did you? Can you? Will you? Won't you? Are you? Aren't you? Why can't you ever? How come you never? Surely you realize! How many times do I have to tell you?"

THE LANGUAGE OF LOVE

When we want to speak the language of love, the two sweetest phrases ever uttered in English to show a genuine interest in the response are. "What was your understanding of what happened?" and, "Let me be sure I understand."

The other great phrases in the language of love are, What? Where? When? and How? These questions are effective when used not as an interrogatory but as a genuine invitation to share or explore experiences and meaning.

The key, again, is attitude. We can notice how much our tone of voice changes when we go from assuming and expecting to asking, "what," "why," and "how" with genuine interest?

Children will double their resistance when they sense our attitude is, "I'm going to use all my resources to manipulate this person to do it the way I want them to."

If our attitude conveys, "I am going to be open to whatever I sense and get in touch with, or understand, this child's point of view," then we invite dialogue and cooperation.

BUILD ON IMPROVEMENT

We are more effective in encouraging young people when we celebrate what goes well when they open up even a little. We can learn to be comfortable with what they do communicate to us and look at what went right. That is seeing the glass of water as half full instead of half empty, when we are celebrating any little movement in the right direction.

FRIENDSHIP AND LOVE — IMPOSSIBLE WITHOUT DIALOGUE

Is it possible to build a friendship with anyone without a meaningful exchange of perceptions with an attitude of genuine interest in the response?. We can't do it.

When we court, what do we do? We spend hours and hours in dialogue, act incredibly interested, and create something beautiful called love. Then if we are not careful, we marry, cut out the dialogue, substitute expectations, begin the business of marriage together, and ruin the relationship. If we ever want to rebuild the marriage we must go back to dialogue.

Three perceptions are necessary before closeness and trust can be established in a relationship:

1. This person is listening to me.

2. I can risk my perceptions and feelings here without being discounted for them.

3. This person's behavior toward me indicates that what I think or have to offer is significant.

Without these three things, I don't trust you, I don't believe what you say, and I hide from you.

THE MEANING OF LOVE

Until we believe that we are listened to, taken seriously, and most of all, are significant in a relationship; it has no value to us.

If you tell me you love me, but don't listen to me, discount my perceptions and feelings, and make the mistake of doing everything for me so that I feel totally irrelevant around you, I will resent you for saying you love me. However, if you listen to me, treat my perceptions and feelings with respect, and affirm the significant things that I am needed for in the relationship, I will know you respect me and care deeply in your own way, even if you never tell me you love me. I will know that in your eyes I am worth something.

ADULTISMS

We have observed that American families, with all the things competing for available time, have developed a very lazy, unproductive pattern of dealing with each other in the time they spend together. Watch how many times this week you find yourself, in allegedly intimate relationships that are important to you and your support system, dealing with those that you love this way:

"Did you? Can you? Do you? Will you? Won't you? Are you? Aren't you?" These questions can all be responded to with a harrump, a shrug, a grump, or nothing.

"Did you have a good day?" "I don't know." "Did that work out all right?" "I don't know." "Is everything all right?" "I don't know."

It is also the language of disrespect. It says, "I am going to reduce you to a multiple choice animal. You can pick the options I have chosen, but I am not going to invest much time into finding out what really happened in your life."

BRINGING DIALOGUE BACK

No culture ever pre-empted more dialogue than we have in the past 30 to 40 years. We can bring it back.

The first step necessary to bring dialogue back is to stop creating the barriers and using the multiple choice/true or false language of disrespect.

The second step is to start using the language of respect through the EIAG (what, why, how) process.

The third step is to be patient while children get used to the new climate this change will create.

A THREATENING ATMOSPHERE IS A BARRIER TO DIALOGUE

Conditional love, approval, and acceptance creates a threatening atmosphere which eliminates dialogue.

> "Whenever a person perceives threat in any environment, including the real or imagined loss of regard, the possibility of rejection, or the possibility of feeling foolish; he or she will stop learning and practice self-defense. He or she will lie, scapegoat, cheat, or do anything that keeps the threatening person from seeing him or her as he or she is."
>
> Kurt Lewin

> "Until I can risk appearing imperfect in your eyes, without fear that it will cost me something, I can't really learn from you."
>
> Rudolph Dreikurs

Dreikurs and Lewin were aware of the habits we often acquire that interfere with our ability to help our children and others feel significant and acceptable to us.

We have identified three basic behaviors that create a threatening atmosphere.

1. The use of kids' grades as their identity.

2. Rewarding their achievement with love and expressions of praise and affection.

3. Giving generic praise and approval rather than specific insight.

When we take the time to give *specific feedback* we affirm the contribution of others. Generic praise does not affirm. Specific recognition always affirms. This means taking the time to recognize what was done well.

The language of recognition is: I feel _____ about _____ because _____. "I feel pleased about having the kitchen cleaned because it is nicer to cook in a clean kitchen," or "I feel upset that the kitchen is not cleaned up because it is very unpleasant to cook in a messy kitchen."

This response not only gives clear feedback, it is more trustworthy. How do you feel when a teacher returns a paper marked *great*! but does not include any specific feedback, as opposed to a paper that includes a comment, "I really like the way your paragraphs were organized."

THE ART OF AFFIRMATION VS. PRAISE

An affirmation contains specific elements of recognition. It requires noticing the specific things other do that are effective and affirming those specific things in order to start the process of affirmation in a genuine way.

When we say, "Terrific!", or "Great!" others may not trust that non-specific type of praise. When we say, "That is a terrific idea because _____," and then tell exactly what we like about it, others know that our words are thoughtfully related to what others have done.

Many people believe that if we say *good* things and give others lots of praise, they will do better. In reality, they may become more fearful, dependent, and vulnerable.

The problem with praise is that it is effective in making people dependent upon the approval or opinion of others. Praise encourages an outer locus of control.

THE PRESSURE TO PERFORM

Kids who believe that our love, praise, or affection is contingent upon them pleasing us and doing what we want become the most vulnerable of all people when they can't deliver for some reason and are desperate not to lose that love.

We found recently that 94% of all teachers and 98% of all parents use negative management strategies with children in the classroom and in the home. Detailed criticism for unacceptable work, generic praise or approval for success, which has only the capacity to raise people to mediocrity, gives them no opportunity to transcend into self-actualization.

PLEASERS AND APPROVAL JUNKIES

Personal criticism and generic praise teaches young people to work for approval rather than insight and understanding and to take errors as a reflection of negative personal worth. We have trained teachers to put round smiley faces, A pluses, and vacuous comments like *terrific*! on school papers. After the age of 10 these are counter productive strategies.

SPECIFIC FEEDBACK

If we want to help others grow and to gain the tools to self-actualize and succeed, it is important to tell them specifically what we liked about what they did, so they understand the criteria and know we actually understood what they did.

To say, "This is a great paper because these footnotes were well documented. I have underscored a couple that I think you could use as a model for next time. I believe your thesis statement was clear, and you outlined the rest of your paper very well, and I've underlined a couple of sentences that I thought were particularly effective," gives the student specifics that can be held up against the next paper for comparison. It will also prepare students to go to work and to go to college where professors won't give smiley faces, but will demand performance.

The tendency in our culture to be specific in our criticism, but generic in our approval has taught young people to downgrade approval but to always be waiting for and sensitive to criticism and to believe that the ultimate act is to avoid any criticism and get only approval.

We can separate the children from grades by saying something like, "Son, I am unhappy with the way your report card came out. I don't believe it reflects the kind of effort you could have put in. I'm very interested to know what you believe produced the report card as you have it now and what you believe it will take to change that in the next semester."

UNCONDITIONAL ACCEPTANCE AND APPROVAL

Not only does this attitude separate the child from the grade, it gives specific feedback and explores his perceptions by offering him the opportunity to clarify what produced the lower level of work and what it will take to correct it.

To say, "What is your understanding of what happened? What is your understanding of why this is an important issue for us? Since this has come up, I need to know what you intend to do, or are willing to do, to correct the situation," invites collaboration and the chance to contribute something. This leaves openings for understanding instead of a dumping ground for *set* perceptions.

To further collaboration and the development of an inner locus of control, after offering our own perception, we can invite the perception of the child. "I basically liked what you handed in, but I would be interested to know what you believe is special about it." This invites a meaningful exchange.

PLAYING THE ODDS

Research has shown that families who organized themselves with rituals, traditions, and activities in the midst of their busy lifestyle to increase the base of informal dialogue among family members by as little as 30 minutes average a week (4 minutes a day) enjoy a 32% lower rate of delinquency, a 27% lower rate of chemical dependency, and a 21% lower rate of chronic truancy, absenteeism, and identified underachievement in their children than identical families on the same street, going to the same schools, but who were at or below the national average in activities that produce dialogue.

MORE THAN WORDS

We need to make it very clear that dialogue is not limited to communication through words. Dialogue takes place when there is a meaningful exchange of perceptions in a climate of support, safety, or understanding. You can communicate a lot with a nod. Being open to the significance of silences can be very important.

Everyday we see friends and say, "You seem a little down. Is everything okay?" We are letting them know that they are communicating something with their posture and their attitude. And, being open to that, we are receiving their messages.

Dialogue can occur in many forms when we are open to the exchange. We encourage dialogue when we stop asking close ended questions such as, "Did you have a good day?" and instead ask, "What things happened to you today?"

If we do say, "How was your day?" and the reply is, "Okay." we can show that we really care by asking, "What was the most okay thing that happened?" or "What does okay mean?"

If it seems that dialogue is not working because our children do not want to participate, we might need to ask ourselves what you might be doing to create resistance. It could also be that we are not creating resistance, but we are not being sensitive to the dialogue styles of our children. Some people like to talk a lot, and some people don't. Some people are simply slower to respond than others, so we need to be more patient. Perhaps we are not being sensitive to non-verbal cues and body language.

Resistance occurs most often when children perceive that we are not really interested, or that we are being threatening in any way, and will possibly use any information we get to criticize or condemn in some way.

Sometimes questions come as an interrogative leading to an inquisition, and that is not dialogue. It has to be an invitation. It can't be coercive.

SUMMARY

The collaborative experiences of contributing through meaningful roles, family rituals, and traditions, plus dialogue about these experiences are the primary means to affirm young people with the perceptions of meaning, purpose, and significance.

Chapter 6

HELPING CHILDREN DEVELOP A PERCEPTION OF HAVING CONTROL OVER THEIR ENVIRONMENT

The third of the *significant seven*, developing a strong perception of having control or influence over events and experiences in one's life, builds on the first two of the *significant seven*.

The first two of the *significant seven* will help people begin to be more confident that they do effect circumstances in their lives through their actions, choices, and thinking. But now we are looking specifically at peoples' beliefs about the role they play in what happens in life.

One characteristic of high-risk individuals is that they do not perceive themselves as having a significant amount of ability to affect what happens to them in their life. They believe in fate or luck and frequently experience impotence and powerlessness in their life.

LOCUS OF CONTROL

We call this variable, from a research standpoint, locus of control. Understanding locus of control is a way of measuring whether people are inner or outer directed. Successful people have a predominately internal locus of control. Victims, who chronically struggle, have an external locus of control.

EXTERNAL LOCUS OF CONTROL

Having an *external* locus of control describes a person who would prescribe to the following description of reality: "It doesn't matter much what people do, things either work out or they don't. What happens is simply a matter of good or bad luck.

I have no control over what happens to me. People do things to me that I don't necessarily deserve, but what happens to me is largely a result of environment and what others do to me."

People who have an external locus of control are more easily influenced by the opinions of others, both to give them a sense of their own worth and to tell them what to do. Young people are more easily influenced by peer pressure. These are the people more likely to become pleasers and approval junkies and who become depressed when they do not live up to their perceived expectation of others. They depend on things outside themselves for happiness such as material possessions, success as interpreted by others, or being loved by someone else. Many have a sense of competition and feel they can achieve approval only if they are better than someone else and often criticize and put others down.

INTERNAL LOCUS OF CONTROL

Having an *internal* locus of control describes a person who believes the opposite and has the perception that "What happens to me is largely a result of the decisions that I make and the effort that I put forth. I believe that I can usually find a way to work out a problem. I believe that by talking to people, I can solve problems or develop better relationships. I believe there's a correlation between what I do and what happens to me, between the effort that I put forth and the rewards that I enjoy from life. When I can't influence what happens, I can still decide how I will let circumstances effect me!"

People who have an internal locus of control believe that *the kingdom of heaven is within*. They can enjoy the approval of others and material possessions, but they don't depend on them for their happiness. Their happiness comes from within, through a sense of gratitude for the miracles of life, peace of mind, compassion, and love for others. They feel successful from within and bring that feeling to anything they do.

People with an external locus of control usually take one of three paths through life. They either feel depressed most of the time because of their sense of failure in finding success and happiness outside themselves; or they run a *tread mill* all their lives with an eternal hope that someday they will find it *out there*; or they live a life of rebellion trying to find a pseudo sense of power.

Dr. Wayne Dyer tells a delightful story on his cassette tape series, Choosing Your Own Greatness: One day an old alley cat wandered by an interesting sight. He observed a young alley cat running around and around trying to catch its own tail. He watched in fascination for hours. When the young alley cat finally stopped to catch his breath, the old alley cat asked, "Would you mind telling me what you are doing?"

The young alley cat said, "Certainly. I went to Cat Philosophy School and learned that happiness is in our tails. I am going to keep chasing my tail because someday I will catch it and get a big bite of happiness."

The old alley cat said, "Well, I have never been to Cat Philosophy School, but I know it is true that happiness is in our tails. However, I have found that when I just wander around enjoying life, it follows me everywhere I go."

This story is not meant to imply that people with an internal locus of control *just wander around enjoying life*. People with an inner locus of control bring a sense of joy to whatever they do and thus are successful at whatever they do.

CONDITIONS WHICH ENCOURAGE A BELIEF IN EXTERNAL LOCUS OF CONTROL

The idea that a nuclear bomb may explode at any moment is a good excuse for many to say, "What can I do?"

Every generation for all time has been faced with its own imminent mortality, usually a lot closer to home. In early times there was never certainty that Dad would return home from the hunt. Pioneers, Indians, and the environment were constantly destroying each other. Older generations were constantly threatened by diseases that could destroy whole communities or individuals.

People in our society are constantly encouraged to give up their internal locus of control to drugs such as tranquilizers, aspirin, and alcohol. The message is, "Don't use your own resources to solve a problem; just dull your senses so the problem won't bother you so much."

DEVELOPING AN INTERNAL OR EXTERNAL LOCUS OF CONTROL

Parenting that includes rescuing, enabling, and the other barriers we have discussed in previous chapters tends to reinforce the perception in children of an external locus of control.

Modeling is also important. We can be strong or weak models for our children in this area. We model a belief in an external locus of control when we come home from work and blame others for every difficult situation we have encountered that day.

We model a belief in an internal locus of control when we say, "A very difficult situation is going on for me at work, and *I haven't decided what I am going to do about it yet*."

A mother who says, "Do something with my child," is not

going to improve because she perceives herself as powerless and is looking outside herself for a solution to the problem. If we can help her change her beliefs so she says, "Help me learn what to do differently with this child," she will have accepted the perception that her locus of control lies within herself. She will then be more likely to bring about a successful solution to her problem.

Successful people see *situations*. Unsuccessful people see *problems*. The following verse captures the differences between internal and external locus of control:

The winner is always part of the answer;
The loser is always part of the problem;
The winner always has a program;
The loser always has an excuse;
The winner says, "Let me do it for you;"
The loser says, "That is not my job;"
The winner sees an answer for every problem;
The loser sees a problem for every answer;
The winner sees a green near every sand trap;
The loser sees two or three sand traps near every green;
The winner say, "It may be difficult, but it is possible";
The loser says, "It may be possible, but it is too difficult".

BE A WINNER!

How do young people develop perceptions of being a winner or a loser? It begins with parental practices of threatening, correcting, directing, and expecting well beyond the capacity of children which give them perceptions that, "I am a hopeless pawn and what happens to me in life is what other people do to me."

THE BOOB TUBE STRIKES AGAIN

An external locus of control is reinforced by television which continuously portrays the five themes listed in Chapter Two: the notion that life is a matter of fate, luck, magic, and instant gratification and that even the most complex mess in human life should have a happy ending, or at least be easily solved within the time span of a 60 second commercial or the time span of a single program. Television encourages children to believe that solutions are instantaneous and miraculous and that results are usually obtained through some external product or service, that drinking and casual sex are the primary social activities.

A great deal of research has indicated that the more television people watch, the more pessimistic they become about life. They also tend to see themselves as *victims* of events and circumstances more than actors upon these elements of life circumstances.

We have found a decreasing decline in the tolerance within young people for the notion of persevering until they work things out. Many go into marriage with the perception that if they are not happy immediately, they can trade in the marriage and move on to something else. "Doesn't anyone stay together anymore?" is a line from a popular song today.

Family counselors are reporting a great resistance among younger clients to the notion of enduring some unhappiness and some unpleasantness while using patience, effort, and commitment to work on problems in relationships.

MEAN WHAT YOU SAY AND SAY WHAT YOU MEAN

When we add two other common parental practices, we end up in serious difficulty. Many parents say things such as, "You're grounded forever," and then let children go out, or "If you do that, I'll just die," and then they don't die!

Parents who promise their children that they will just die, ought to keep their promise and drop dead. Think of all the credibility we would gain if we would drop dead when we said we would. On the other hand, imagine how disillusioning it is to a child when we promise them something and don't deliver. Then children know they can't trust what their parents say.

SETTING LIMITS

Many parents pamper their children *in the name of love*. The truth is that pampering is one of the most unloving things we can do to our children. When things come easily for children, they grow up thinking the *world owes them a living*. When we give in to children when they hassle us, we are teaching them to put all their intelligence and energy into learning how to manipulate others into taking care of them, instead of learning to take care of themselves.

It is not love to let a people off the hook so they do not have to experience limits and consequences that were reasonably set and agreed upon.

We set unreasonable limits with our children because we often wait until after something has gone wrong to decide what we'll do about it. When we have failed to anticipate what was likely to happen, we often react with anger and say things like, "You'll never go out again as long as you live if you are late again."

A STITCH IN TIME SAVES NINE

We save ourselves a great deal of aggravation when we use our wisdom and experience to anticipate possible problems and plan for them in advance, as in the following conversation:

"Honey, is there any possible reason why you might be delayed tonight?"

"No, I don't believe there is."

"Then, since there isn't any reason for that to happen, I'll expect you to be home on time. If you decide not to be home on time and come home late, then I'm going to require you to stay home for the next week and not go out at all in order for you to understand that the privilege of going out is based upon the responsibility of being home on time."

If the child chooses to come home at a time other than the agreed to time, it is not necessary or effective to get angry. It can be handled with friendly firmness, dignity, and respect.

"Honey, I'm sorry that you decided to handle it this way, but I've got to respect your decision to stay home for the rest of the week. "

The child may act confused and object, "I don't understand. What do you mean, *my* decision?"

Then you can say, "Well, as we agreed, you could either be home on time or in making the decision not to be home on time, make the decision not to go out at all for the next week. I'm sorry to see that you made the decision to come home late and in doing that, made the decision to not go out at all for the rest of the week."

When children come home late from an agreed-to curfew, it is best to avoid the adultisms that often come to mind: "You know better than that. How can you be so irresponsible? If you are going to act like a child, then you will be treated like a child."

A more effective approach is: "Honey, what was your understanding of what we agreed to on your curfew?"

A child might honestly be confused, and say, "I'm not sure, Dad."

This is an opportunity for clarification: "Since you're not sure, that would explain why we've had this problem. Let me refresh on my understanding of what we agreed upon. It is my understanding that you would be home at twelve, and if anything happened that would prevent you from being home at twelve, you would call us to let us know what had taken place. Do you recall that?"

"I remember that now, Dad."

"What was your understanding of what we agreed would happen if you decided not to be home at twelve?"

"Well, I'd have to stay home for the rest of the week."

"I just wanted to be sure we both had the same understanding about why you won't be going out for the rest of the week."

This is so much better than, "Okay, for you, you little sucker, that's it for this week. I'm going to fix your wagon forever!"

PLEASE HASSLE ME

We may not realize how we invite the hassling from children that then irritates us so much. We do this by setting limits we don't respect and threatening children with things that we don't deliver. We often say things we don't mean, like, "I can't afford it." What does "I can't afford it" mean to children who have never had to do without any of their essential needs and have found that most of the things that they want come fairly easily?

When my daughter says she wants a new bicycle, and I say I can't afford it, she wonders, "What on earth could Daddy be saying to me?"

She reflects on her experience and remembers, "The last three times Daddy said that he couldn't afford it, I hassled him until I got what I wanted. So he must mean that I haven't hassled him enough for him to make this a priority."

So I say, "I can't afford it."

And she says, "Hassle, hassle."

I reassure her, "No, dear, I really can't afford it this time."

And she says, "Hassle, hassle, hassle."

Finally I say, "Look, the only way I can consider it is on my credit card, and it is full."

She thinks, "Now we're making progress. He's considering ways to get it for me. I'm very close." So she continues to hassle.

My last weapon is to say, "If I get this for you, you'll have to give up your allowance for three years."

She thinks to herself, "Well, last time I gave it up for two years and still haven't done without a nickel one day in my life, so that's no big deal."

So she proceeds with hassle, hassle, hassle. I give in, get the bicycle, and she rides off into the setting sun.

What is her perception of how you get what you want? Wish for it, hassle for it long enough, and you can even overcome, "I can't afford it."

GUIDELINES

So now we have established some new guidelines. If we want our children to perceive the power that they have over their life, we need to tell them the truth. We should not say, "I can't afford it," unless we really can't afford it. If we mean, "You haven't hassled me enough to make it a priority," then we need to be honest. That way they can hassle us with dignity and respect and in the end understand why it was that hassling produced the outcome they desired.

We need to set reasonable limits in advance, and then respect them when we have set them. We should not threaten them with things that we can't or won't deliver. That way they understand how their world is organized.

We should not say to them, "You are grounded forever," or, "You can't go out this weekend," unless there is no possible condition that would result in them going out. We need to stop and think about our position. If what we really mean is, "The way I feel right now it is unlikely you will get to go out. Butter me up a little and I might change my mind," we can say that honestly.

We can structure responsibilities and privileges around the home to further reinforce their perception of the control they have over their life.

In future chapters we will look at developing self- discipline and responsibility as important ways to reinforce their perception of how they affect and control things in their lives. The basic message is to have children see the relationship between cause and effect in their lives and have confidence in their ability to affect things.

We can teach children to believe that discussing a problem with someone may result in a better solution. If we leave no room for dialogue and negotiation and our behavior says to them that what they do has no influence on what happens in the family, then that reinforces the messages of a world that would have them believe that things like self-discipline, judgement, and responsibility have no relevance at all to a person who sees himself as powerless and a victim of his environment.

We can help young people cultivate the perception that they have some power to affect their life, that the decisions they make have a reasonable chance of affecting their lives, and that by putting forth the effort, trying, thinking, they can make a difference in what happens to them.

A person does not have to be given power and does not have to actually experience a great deal of independence in order to develop this perception of power and independence. What it takes is someone committed to exploring the what, the why, and the how of our experiences and not assuming that because a child has had an experience of influencing something that they understand how they did that.

So we have to be careful that limits are set in the home, that dialogue takes place between us in ways that clearly convey what we have agreed to. We can be open to a certain amount of negotiation when we are *setting* the limits, but not when we are applying those limits.

STRICTNESS AND PERMISSIVENESS

A number of parenting practices increase young peoples' sense of powerlessness. Strictness, which is excessive manipulation or control by others, causes people to feel powerless and frustrated. When children do not believe they have power over their environment and what happens to them, they often seek power in destructive ways. Excessive strictness trains young people to *give-in* or rebel.

Permissiveness produces insecurity and the belief that there is very little cause and effect in life except to wing it and try to manipulate circumstances as they come along. Permissiveness trains young people to use their resources to manipulate other people into their service.

EPAC

In Chapter Eleven we discuss an instrument called EPAC which can predict the probability of delinquency, underachievement, and drug use for young people, and even the drug of choice, based on the kind of parenting they receive. The extremes of strictness and permissiveness are both dangerous. The most effective parenting to develop capable young people is firmness with dignity and respect which is a combination of loving control designed to help children move toward loving autonomy.

Many parents and teachers are afraid to give up their controlling, authoritarian methods because they believe the only alternative is irresponsible permissiveness. Other parents and teachers are afraid to give up their permissiveness because they believe the only alternative is hostile tyranny.

All of the concepts we discuss in this book are based on the premise of firmness with dignity and respect. Firmness with dignity and respect maintains control and responsibility but quickly brings children along to share in both the control and the responsibility.

This accomplishes two goals. It helps children develop the significant seven perceptions and capabilities, and it makes parenting and teaching easier over the long run. As one teacher said, "Learning to use these methods has relieved me of the despised roles of policeman, judge, jury, and executioner. Now I have time to teach."

One of the many ways this is accomplished is through natural and logical consequences which are dealt with in Chapter Nine.

FAMILY MEETINGS

Family meetings, emphasized in the previous chapter as a way to create a meaningful role for young people, can also be an effective process to help young people develop perceptions of having control over their environment. Successful family meetings are based on the premise of total family involvement so everyone feels needed and significant. Problems cannot be solved without feelings of closeness, trust, and cooperation.

Family meetings are not only for solving problems. Their main purpose is to teach family members a process of working together in ways that are beneficial to the total family unit as well as to each individual. The fact that they can be the most effective way to solve problems in the process is a fringe benefit.

CONTROL OVER THINGS THAT HAPPEN

An important part of the family meeting process is having an agenda displayed prominently where all family members can note the things they would like to discuss. A piece of paper under a magnet on the refrigerator is a popular place. Young people develop perceptions of having control over their environment when they know they can decide on things they would like discussed or that their input is important in deciding on issues other family members would like to discuss.

WE ARE IN THIS TOGETHER

Family meetings are successful only when decisions are made by consensus. This further enhances perceptions of significance and having control over things that happen through cooperation and negotiation.

When the family cannot reach total agreement on a situation, that item should be tabled for a week or however long it takes to reach a consensus. In the family of one of the authors, the item of owning a dog was tabled for six months. The children wanted a dog. The parents did not. The parents presented their concerns that they would be left with all the responsibility to feed the dog and clean up all the messes. The children assured them that they would take full responsibility. The parents finally conceded when the children agreed to the consequences that the dog would be given away if the children did not keep their commitment to take full responsibility. A month later the dog was given away because the children did not keep their promises. This was a very difficult lesson even though it was carried out with firmness, dignity, and respect.

For six more months they continued to discuss owning a dog before the parents agreed to try again. The children were very diligent in taking care of this dog because they knew their parents would stick to their agreed upon consequences of giving the dog away if they didn't.

It is important for adults to realize that some issues must be discussed over and over. We discuss the issue of chores in our family about every three weeks. The children will enthusiastically follow the plan they come up with for doing their chores for about two or three weeks before their enthusiasm dims. When *chores* shows up on the agenda again, they might devise another plan or simply decide to use the old plan with renewed commitment.

Many single parents wonder if they should have family meetings. The benefits are the same no matter how many or how few people are in a family.

Young people, as well as adults, are much more motivated to follow plans in which they have ownership because of dialogue and collaboration. They feel significant and potent when they are involved in important decisions that affect them.

Family meetings are an excellent way of compensating for the lack of the need for children in our present economic structure. When we don't find ways of using their talents in productive ways, they often become *victims* of affluence.

AFFLUENCE

When parents provide everything for their children, and do everything for them, children are robbed of developing skills and capabilities that help them develop an internal locus of control and the ability to be independent.

We are now finding that parents make a serious mistake when they provide *first class* living for their children without creatively involving their children in the cost of going first class. Wise parents provide *economy class accommodations* and then charge tolls in time and effort when children want more.

When my children want jeans, I am willing to provide for good solid basics. Today, however, many young people expect more than basics. They want *style*, which is determined by designer labels. The other day my daughter rushed up to me and said, "Daddy I need some Calvin Klein and Guess Jeans."

I replied, "Listen honey, I got into the parenting deal to cover your body, not to decorate it, and I've discovered I can cover it for about $18."

She was horrified, "Dad, I can't wear $18 jeans. They're generic to the max. Don't be a terminal nerd."

I've learned humility, so I replied, "I don't understand that. What I understand is that there are wants and there are needs. What you want is style; what you need is modesty. Frankly, I am only committed to modesty because I can handle that for eighteen dollars. When you ask me to consider style, you are asking for twenty five dollars more. I have the money. That is not the issue. The issue is what you are asking me to do to my priorities. You are asking me to place designer jeans ahead of long-term, tax-sheltered retirement for your mom and myself. You are asking me to ignore the possibility of my offspring becoming so inspired with self-improvement that they might need tuition for higher education. You are asking me to ignore rising energy costs and other exigencies that could unexpectedly rock the family boat this fall. Instead of developing a little hedge now to put us on top of all that, you are asking me to throw all that aside and go for style."

"Now, honey, you are asking me to line up designer jeans ahead of energy costs, tuition, and retirement. The only way I can provide for those exigencies and still come up with style would be to make other adjustments in my life, such as parking the car and walking to work for several days to save gas money and to pass up lunch for a few days. It occurs to me that if you went without lunch for a few days, the jeans might fit better when you got them anyway."

"But you are working hard, and you keep assuring me that you are mature and able to take initiative in your life. You always ask me for privileges based on that premise. So, I would be real impressed if you came to me and said, 'Dad, this meant enough to me that, even though it is embarrassing for me in my senior year, I parked the car and rode the school bus to save gas money. I passed up two chances to go to multi-cinemas with my friends on the weekend. I went without snacks for a week, and I have saved half the difference. Would you meet me half way?'"

"If it is not worth that kind of sacrifice to you, and it definitely is not worth that to me; why don't we go with modesty now, and be done with it? That is reasonable isn't it?"

A few weeks later my daughter rushed up to me, and said accusingly, "Dad you have new ostrich boots."

I said, "Exactly. And I put in a fair bit of extra time and effort to enjoy them. I am not fundamentally opposed to enjoying nice things; I'm just fundamentally opposed to being the only one in the family who must put forth the extra time and effort and comprise priorities so that you can enjoy them. I guess I lived with the fantasy that I had four children in the naive view that they would one day support me in a fashion to which I was willing to become accustomed. Since that dream may not come true, I'm willing to share the first class journey, but I am not willing to carry you in style. I am willing to walk with you, but you have strong legs and you can use them."

I am not talking about neglect. I am talking about weaning. And remember that weaning has never been attractive to the *weaner* or the *weanee*. But it has always been essential to the survival of both, and that is really important now.

Television watching is one area where extensive weaning would be beneficial toward the development of capable people.

SUBSTITUTES FOR TELEVISION

Television watching is one routine that could be discussed during a family meeting. We have discussed how harmful the influence of television can be when children are overly exposed to the five themes of television: self-medication, drinking, casual sexuality, expedient acts of violence, and miraculous solutions to problems within the short time span.

Most families do not devise a plan for watching television. Instead they just have the television on most of the time and watch whatever happens to be showing at the time. People will often switch stations over and over again looking for something decent to watch, but when they can't find anything *good* they simply watch the best of the worst.

It would be much better to decide during a family meetings how much television will be allowed. We suggest one to three hours per day, with flexibility for special programs. Since most children watch six to eight hours of television a day, this would be a real improvement. During a planning session allow children to choose from a television guide which programs they "really" want to watch, and then keep the television off the rest of the time. If you have only one television set and different members of the family want to watch different programs, develop a plan for compromise. Perhaps each member can have first choice on different days.

We also suggest that you sit and watch some programs with your children and discuss their perceptions of what they have seen after the program.

It is also important to involve the family in planning for other things to do during the time they have been used to watching television. It can be very scary for everyone to simply announce, "We are no longer going to watch so much television." This can cause a real panic about what else is there to do? When people have not been used to taking with each other, being together without the distraction of the television can be very awkward at first.

One mother gathered her children and the neighborhood children outside and taught them to play some of the group games she once played as a child such as *Kick The Can* and *Hide and Seek*.

Other families have planned to play Monopoly and other board games, play charades, take trips to the library, listen to motivational tapes and then discuss them, read classic books out loud, or do exercises together.

Remember to focus on things *to do* rather than what *not to do*.

Family meetings can be used for planning family routines and events such as vacations and schedules for use of the family car.

Involving young people in family meetings is an excellent way to give them experience and practice in having a voice in what happens to them which can give them strong perceptions of having control over their environment.

LIMITS AND CONSEQUENCES ENCOURAGE A BELIEF IN INTERNAL LOCUS OF CONTROL.

When we don't allow people to affect things in their lives and hold them accountable for their actions and the results of their actions, then we reinforce the perception that, "It's fate when I don't make it, luck when I do, but either way there was little that I had to do with it."

By avoiding the *barriers* and using the *builders* described in Chapter Four, we also encourage people to see their own influence over their life.

Even the EIAG principles emphasized in the previous chapters are very effective when focused on individual actions, choices, and efforts:

"What caused you to do that?"
"What other options did you have?"
"How do you plan to deal with the situation now?"

These are excellent questions that reflect a belief in other people's potency or influence over their life experiences. When young people sense our belief in them through our use of the EIAG process and the other activities explained in this chapter, they will feel the support that can be so important in helping them develop a perception of having control over their environment.

HELPING CHILDREN DEVELOP STRONG INTRA-PERSONAL SKILLS

The fourth of the *significant seven* helps children develop strong skills for handling their inner feelings, thoughts, and emotions in ways that help them enjoy successful living.

THE THREE PRIMARY INTRA-PERSONAL SKILL

1. Self-assessment

2. Self-control

3. Self-discipline

SELF-ASSESSMENT

Self-assessment means the ability to interpret, recognize, and acknowledge personal feelings such as frustration, anger, joy, happiness, excitement and love. This capability requires the development of a vocabulary to express these feelings. The language necessary to express the well-developed intra-personal skill of self-assessment begins with "I." "I am excited, I am upset, I am frustrated, I am angry."

ENCOURAGING SELF-ASSESSMENT

Self-assessment is a skill that can be developed, and the necessary vocabulary can be learned. Adults can help by asking questions that invite self-assessment: "What do you think? What did that mean to you? How do you feel about that? How was that important to you?"

Self-assessment is discouraged when parents say, "We don't get angry! We don't yell! Go to your room right now, if you can't control yourself!" Telling young people what they can and can't feel teaches them to deny their emotions or hide them, instead of experiencing their emotions within reasonable limits.

Parents who say, "Control yourself," have often lost control of their own emotions. Otherwise they could observe with empathy what the child is experiencing and give gentle guidance where needed rather than getting caught up in their child's emotions.

Empathetic observation and gentle guidance might be expressed as follows: "I don't blame you for being angry. I would be too. I can't let you hit your sister, but I will talk with you about it in a little while when you've settled down and feel a little better." This example shows how we can allow children to experience their feelings as legitimate, give them feedback, yet set limits on how their feelings may be expressed.

The empathic parent models self-assessment, self-control, and self-discipline by refusing to use unproductive time (when the emotions are out of control) to discuss and deal with the emotions.

The worst time to teach about anger is when anyone is angry. The best time is after the experience: Close enough to recall the emotion, but far enough away to be objective and not get caught up in the anger again.

Treating children's emotions as legitimate and giving them access to ours can be done with expressions such as, "I'm feeling too angry to talk right now. I need to take a walk, I'll talk with you later when I've calmed down." We replace blame with feelings by omitting *you*. We are not taking responsibility for our own feelings when we say, "You made me angry. You made me upset."

We emphasize the *situation* and our own *responsibility* when we say, "I'm really angry about what has happened, so this is not a good time to talk about it. When I have thought about it some more I will come and find you."

We need to let children see our emotions and let them be involved to the extent that they can without putting responsibility on them and without denying those feelings and emotions ourselves.

Whenever we express a valid emotion, we should not apologize for it later by saying, "I'm sorry. I was upset," or, "I'm sorry. I got angry." We model self-control, self-assessment, and self-discipline by acknowledging, "As you could tell, I was very upset over what happened. Now that I have settled down I would like to go over it with you so that we both understand what happened."

On the other hand, if we act inappropriately as a result of our anger and humiliate children and blame them for our anger, it is effective to apologize: "I'm sorry I blamed you for my anger and said some disrespectful things to you. I have calmed down now and would like to discuss the situation rationally and work on some solutions with you." From our example, children can learn when it is appropriate to apologize. An apology when appropriate is part of a process called *Recovery* which is discussed in Chapter Twelve.

Once children become comfortable with the notion that their feelings are a legitimate part of their life, that their feelings are worthy of respect, and that the feelings of others are worthy of respect, they are ready to take the next step.

SELF-CONTROL

Self-control is the ability to select an appropriate response to a feeling from among a number of possible behaviors. It requires the recognition that feelings do not cause actions. Feelings are only feelings. Actions are the choices of the mind on how to respond to the feeling.

ENCOURAGING SELF-CONTROL

An individual can practice by evaluating a previous behavior: "I felt angry. I expressed the anger by hitting. What was the outcome? I was restricted, grounded, got beat up. Next time I'm angry, if I don't want that outcome to occur, what other behaviors are there? What else could I do with that anger besides precipitating a brawl?"

Children develop self-control when we teach them to separate feelings, actions, and outcomes so they learn to understand, "I feel _____ I do _____ I experience _____. Next time I feel a certain emotion I might do something different so that I can experience another outcome."

With little children we can start them out gently and encourage them to understand by asking, "What were you feeling? What did you do? What happened to you?" These questions are designed to help them understand what has already happened. When they are older, they can begin to project into the future.

We know children are ready to project what they have learned into future events when they stop asking, "Is it Saturday yet?" and are able to understand, "It will be Saturday in three days." That is a good time to begin asking, "When you feel ... what could you do, and what is likely to happen?"

When children are still saying, "What day is it? Is this Saturday yet? Is it time to go to the park yet?" they are not thinking abstractly enough to project into the future. We can get them to describe what just happened or what is happening right now, but we cannot require them to explain their feelings or their choices in the middle of a feeling.

Even with older children and spouses it is not a good idea to step in with questions right in the middle of the anger. We will generally promote more anger if we try this. Unless intervention is necessary to prevent clear and present harm, it is better to let the episode develop in its course and then, when children are closer to control, go back over it to help them understand.

As children get older, six through eight years of age, they begin to be capable of learning that their emotions need to be controlled. They can begin to understand that it is not what anger makes them do, but what they choose to do when they are angry that is the significant issue.

As children become adept at generating and selecting from a menu of options and behaviors, they are exhibiting self-control. They are able to impose *self* between the feeling and the action and, therefore, gain control.

Our goal is to help children understand that feelings are legitimate, but the choices they make in handling their feelings and emotions have consequences. When they have this understanding, they are ready to go to the next level, which is self-discipline.

SELF-DISCIPLINE

Self-discipline is the ability to consider an outcome in the abstract and then select a behavior that will achieve it. In short, we could say that self-discipline is the product of self-assessment and self-control in response to a given situation.

The self-assessment part is, "What do I most want to happen out of this experience? How would I like to feel when this is over? What do I desire to have happen as a result of this?" Self-control is understanding which of the behaviors available to me, or that I can imagine, would bring me closest to what I desire to happen?"

The self-discipline part comes when people are able to set aside what they feel like doing in order to get what they need to get done.

ENCOURAGING SELF-DISCIPLINE

Self-discipline is not possible as a truly spontaneous reaction to life until children reach about seven or eight years of age. Before then it is unreasonable to expect them to control their impulses and feelings based on learning or appreciation for others. Children below that age we can teach the consequences of giving in to their feelings through the EIAG process, but we shouldn't expect them to understand, "Even though I feel like hitting someone, I believe that for the long term interest of this relationship it would be best to go down and talk it over." That more mature response is generally not even possible, developmentally, until about eight years of age. After that, the results reflect how much training and reinforcement children have had.

A special kind of awareness is required to train young people. The environment must be structured in such a way that they have the opportunity to deny themselves, bruise their knees, skin their shins, and break their hearts in little ways that aren't lasting in order to learn how to avoid broken necks, broken backs, and big heartaches later in life after not having this kind of experience.

AVOID PAMPERING

The very basic level of teaching self-discipline begins with a mother or a father who is mature enough and who loves his or her child enough to avoid pampering.

We have made the mistake of calling our son and saying, "Mike, it's time to come in now and eat," and then keeping his dinner warm while we continued calling out to him several times until we became annoyed and went out to get him. We compounded the mistake by allowing him to have a nice warm dinner while we lectured him about his inconsiderateness.

If we are to raise a capable child, we will call him for dinner and then go in and eat, clean up the mess, and put what is left away. Later when he comes in and says, "Where's my dinner?" We can say with love and support, "Honey, when it was time to eat, you felt like playing. Now that you feel like eating, it's time to play. So run on back outside and try again in the morning."

If we have the courage to do that, within a couple of days, We'll begin to get self-discipline from our child. The other way, all we'll get is an endurance contest between who can endure hassling the longest.

We are also looking for a school teacher who does not say, "Mike, even though you didn't get your permission slip in for this field trip, go ahead and have a good time, honey, and bring it in on Monday." Allowing children to escape consequences is something we can no longer afford in this world.

We need a teacher who has the courage to say, "Mike, even though you didn't get your permission slip in for this field trip, I hope you get it in next time so that you don't miss that one too."

We need to be tough enough in our love for our children to endure the little discomfort, the temporary upset and heartache, to help them begin to learn the essential lessons of life.

I came home one day recently and my daughter passed me in the hall. "Hi, Daddy! Glad to see you. I'll be back in a little bit to talk." She was very happy and cheerful as she went on down the hallway.

In a few minutes the next daughter came by and did very much the same thing.

Then their Mom came in. "Hi, honey, glad to see you. I've got to do a couple of things. I'll be back in a couple of minutes." I heard her go down the hallway and down the stairway into the family room. I also heard the daughters go down the stairway into the family room.

All of a sudden there was yelling, screaming, pounding feet up the stairs, and doors slamming.

Within a minute my wife came into the bedroom, flopped on the bed and said, "That's it! I'm taking the American Express card and leaving. It's up to you."

I said, "Wow! Something incredible has happened. That family room has got to be a very dangerous place. I'd better check it out."

So I gathered my courage to its highest limit and proceeded to the top of the stairs and went down looking anxiously around me for signs of the problem. And as I came down the stairs and turned into the family room I discovered the problem. The family had been afflicted by a hyperactive washer and dryer matched up against an underdeveloped folding and storage system in the form of several small children. The symptom of the problem was this large pile of laundry stacked on the hide-a-bed in the middle of the family room.

Apparently Mom would come downstairs and see the pile of clothes and become hostile and aggressive. She would confront the children and they would become manipulative and blaming.

I said, "This has got to stop. It's either the hide-a-bed or us. Something has to change at this point."

Tricia and I decided to take the risk of letting the kids be responsible. We went out and bought four different colored clothes hampers and held a workshop on running the washer and dryer and folding clothes so Mom and Dad could get out of the laundry business.

Now it wasn't quite that simple. Once we had held the workshop on running the washer and dryer and everyone had their own hamper, we had to have some dialogue with each child. "Honey, now that we know you can run the washer and dryer and have a basket for your clothes, is there anything that would result in clothing left on the hide-a-bed?"

Each of the children assured us that there was no reason for clothing to be left on the hide-a-bed any more.

We said, "Fine! We will assume that any clothing left on the hide-a-bed now is surplus clothing that you are finished with and We'll gather it up and take it to *Goodwill*."

And we did! That's the important thing. We did! During the next week we gave away several sets of intimate apparel that had been casually left on the hide-a-bed. We gave away half of a new pair of socks. We gave away a Spiderman shirt that was very cherished by a young disciple of Spiderman. But by the end of the week the consensus of the family was: "Mom and Dad are serious and if you want your stuff, you'd better not leave anything in the family room."

The learning continued over the next few weeks. About two weeks later, my middle daughter went through her learning experience.

She said to me, "Daddy, Keri says I smell funny."

I said, "Come over here a minute and let me check this out."

Sniff! "She's right! What could be causing that?"

"I don't know"

"Well, how are things going with your hamper and the washer and dryer?"

"I haven't used that yet."

"Well, that could be part of the problem."

"Well, how do I know when clothes need to be washed? Mom always took care of that before."

There was our problem. Mom always took care of that before. And I said, "Maybe you're too close to understand the problem. Why don't you take your clothes off here, go over and stand in the doorway, get some fresh air, and come back and check them out."

She came back and said, "They smell funny."

"Well, then what are your choices?"

"Well, instead of going out to play, I'd better stay in and get my clothes washed or there won't be anybody to play with anyway." And she learned a lesson.

A few days later, my oldest daughter went through her process. She happened at that time to be in the eighth grade at the top of the heap in Junior High School. The school year was coming to an end. She was in all of her power and glory. Next year, she would be at the bottom of the heap in High School. And so her plan was to kind of capitalize on her power at the last dance of the school year to go out in a blaze of glory.

So she manipulated until she'd conned Dad into buying a dress he could scarcely afford, but Mom would allow. She took it to church, road-tested it, and raised two or three eyebrows so she knew it had the desired power. She was ready.

Her plan was to have her hair done on Friday and had saved up her money from skating for a couple of weeks so she could afford it. She figured with the hair put up and the new dress she would just really knock them in the eye.

So Friday came and she went off to have her hair done, came home to get ready for the dance, and couldn't find her new dress anywhere. She searched around for it and finally found this beautiful dress right where she had left it after church that Sunday in the bottom of the clothes hamper, all mildewed, stained, and blotched. And she couldn't wear it. So off she went to the biggest dance of her life, in a hodgepodge that didn't excite anybody.

The next day she came to me and said, "Daddy, how long can you leave a dress in the hamper before it get mildewed?"

I said, "Well, this time of the year, with wet swimming suits and towels and stuff, that can happen overnight."

"Gee, I didn't know that. Mom always looked after the clothes before. How did I know, Dad? I ruined the dress. I'd better go through there every night and get my stuff out of there or it's all going to get ruined with these little kids around."

And she learned. The learning took place when the children had a chance to affect important things in their life through the decisions that they made or did not make concerning taking care of their own clothes.

PRIVILEGES AND RESPONSIBILITIES

Structuring related responsibilities and privileges encourages the development of self-discipline. It is possible to have self-discipline without being responsible, but it is not possible to be responsible without self-discipline.

Self-discipline means the ability to control what's going on inside. Responsibility is the ability to recognize and understand limits and consequences, privileges, responsibilities, cause and effect in the world.

There are some people who are so self-disciplined, who control themselves so much, that they are irresponsible with their health, with their relationships with people around them. Anorexia is a result of self-discipline. Not sharing feelings is a result of self-discipline. People who use self-discipline in these ways do not anticipate the consequences of all that self- discipline.

Responsibility requires self-discipline and an understanding of cause and effect relationships in the world. Adults can help young people develop effective self-discipline and responsibility by making sure privileges are directly related to the willingness to accept responsibility.

INCREASED RESPONSIBILITY WITH AGE

As children get older they are developmentally ready for more responsibility. Privileges should be given only when they are ready to accept related responsibility.

When my children were three years old they were given very limited privileges regarding bedtime. They could chose which pair of pajamas they wanted to wear. As they got older, around nine years of age, they were allowed to choose their bedtime. They could go to bed anytime they wanted so long as they accepted the responsibility to get up in the morning by themselves — cheerfully — and to get themselves dressed, make their lunches, eat their breakfast, and get to school on time without any interference or hassling from me.

When we discussed this at a family meeting and they agreed that if they didn't follow through on the responsibilities they would lose the privilege of choosing their own bedtime. We also discussed details for increasing the chances of success. They decided on how much time they would need to get ready in the morning and learned to set their own clock radios.

The plan was tested in several ways. It was very difficult for me to keep my mouth shut and let them succeed or fail without interference from me. I found it helpful to take long showers or long walks in the morning so I could avoid the temptation to remind or threaten.

At first, they were so excited about having the privilege that they stayed up until midnight. It didn't take them long to discover how difficult it was to get up cheerfully and fulfill their responsibilities when they had not had enough sleep. They both had to learn the hard way by having the privilege rescinded for awhile when they found they were just too tired to get up one morning. I simply said, "I respect your decision to give up the privilege of choosing your own bedtime for awhile. Let me know when you want to try it again."

Another way to help children develop responsibility is to teach the difference between needs and wants by providing them with their needs and letting them contribute to their wants. Children have been denied the benefits of contributing to the effort to provide for their wants by *super parents*.

THE SUPER PARENT

A whole generation of parents learned patience, self-discipline, sacrifice, delayed gratification, responsibility, and hard work. These parents did not realize the benefits of their hard work. They thought that *super parents* should do everything for their children and thus deprived their children of opportunities to learn essential ingredients for success.

One out of every five parents is secretly going through school again by doing homework for their children, which could explain why the nationwide achievement scores are going down. Children who have parents doing their homework aren't learning anything except how to manipulate their parents. Previously parents did not have time to stay up late typing a paper for children who tearfully apologized for forgetting to mention it was due in the morning.

A single mother recently complained, "I work two jobs and try to make it home to cook for my 19 year old son, who won't shop or do the dishes. What should I do?"

I said, "Take this quarter, make a phone call, and tell your son you won't make it home tonight to cook his dinner."

She was horrified, "But what will happen?"

"I don't know, but I have observed teenagers who became incredibly self-reliant when faced with starvation. I have seen some eat raw bread. Some have opened a can of Spaghettios and eaten them cold."

When we allow children to meet their needs by manipulation and hassling, we set them up for chemical dependency. Any other solution to dealing with life situations requires self-discipline, delayed gratification, sacrifice, and hard work.

Previous generations experienced affirmations and confidence from learning how to contribute and to get things for themselves. The lack of these experiences for our youth today has created a crisis in self-confidence and self-esteem since one of the surest ways to destroy these traits is to do too much for a person.

Ungrateful children and suffering parents have become the

order of the day, and it is traceable to our fascination with materialism. It is time to use our affluence wisely.

We are not talking about neglect. We are talking about weaning, as mentioned in the previous chapter. We should provide basic accommodations for our children and then structure the environment so they put in time and effort that is designed to stretch them, but not break them.

BARRIERS

In summary, there are three primary barriers that discourage children from developing the intra-personal skills of self- assessment, self-control, and self-discipline.

1. *Projecting Feelings Onto Others*

The first barrier is projecting our feelings onto others. We want to emphasize again the tendency of adults to project their feelings onto children: "You make me angry." "You frustrate me." "You get me upset." This model is the opposite of self-assessment and indicates a lack of taking responsibility for one's own feelings, while placing the blame for those feelings elsewhere. The belief that we are responsible for other people's feelings and emotions is too much baggage for most of us to carry through life, yet we often load children up with that burden.

Children who have our feelings projected onto them immediately have permission to project their feelings onto others. As long as others produce our feelings, there is no foundation for self-assessment or self-control, and we can then justify reacting to our environment rather than acting on it.

Wayne Dyer tells the story of a client who came to see him and claimed that her husband gave her an inferiority complex. Dr. Dyer asked, "Oh, how does he do that?"

The client said, "He tells me I am stupid."

Dr. Dyer said, "Well, knowing him, that does not surprise me. That sounds like the kind of thing he would say, but how does that make you stupid?"

She replied, "When he tells me I am stupid, that makes me feel like I am stupid."

Dr. Dyer said, "Does that mean that if he comes home tonight and tells you that you are a car, you will feel like a car?"

The client laughed, "Of course not! I am not a car!"

Dr. Dyer persisted, "Wait a minute. Suppose he brings a

nozzle and wants to pour gasoline in your ear, then will you feel like a car?"

"Of course not," she said with confidence.

Dr. Dyer asked, "Then why do you feel you are stupid just because he says you are?"

No one else can be responsible for how we feel. This lady would refuse to feel like a car no matter what anyone else said, yet she was quick to believe she was stupid at the slightest suggestion from her husband.

FREEDOM IN RESPONSIBILITY

We choose our feelings based upon our perceptions. There is great freedom in that realization. We can choose our feelings, and we can change our feelings when we change our perceptions. It is not valid to say, "You make me angry! You frustrate me!"

It is valid to declare our feelings. "I am angry! I am upset! I'm really pleased. I'm excited." Then our children can begin to share their feelings, too, and get rid of the guilt through which people will manipulate them their whole life as long as they can make another person responsible for their feelings.

2. *Using "Why?" As An Inquisition*

The second primary barrier to developing the intra-personal skills of self-assessment, self-control, and self-discipline is expecting a rationale for feelings: "Why did you do that? Why do you feel that way? Why are you angry? Why are you frustrated? Why are you upset?" A tendency of people in our culture is to demand a rational explanation for a feeling, rather than a rationale for a behavior: "What caused you to behave that way when you were angry? What were you trying to accomplish when you did that?"

Many variables would have to be looked at before an accurate answer could be given. Every human being ever born wants to know "why," but never wants to be asked "why" with respect to their feelings and their behaviors.

We don't usually know fully *why* we feel something. We may not know *why* we did something, but we can usually say what we were hoping to accomplish. We may not know *why* we have a feeling, but we may be able to say *what* we are feeling. If we allow others to describe feelings and then explore a rationale for their behavior, we can begin to teach them how to modify their behavior to achieve a different outcome or produce a different result, which leads to the third barrier.

We can help young people learn to describe or state a feeling and then look at ideas that separate feels from action: "Next time you are upset like that, what else might you do?"

3. *Doing Too Much for Children*

The third barrier to developing self-discipline is characteristic of super parents who do too much for children. Rescuing and enabling means to rescue people from their inadequacies by compensating for them ourselves or by stepping in and deferring the consequences of their chosen behavior so that they cannot learn to accurately anticipate outcomes.

A child may not feel like getting out of bed in the morning and therefore won't have time to make a lunch. Arriving at school without lunch should result in the child missing lunch. This experience could be followed up with a discussion later about what could be done differently tomorrow morning when the child feels like sleeping in if he wants to have lunch that day. The child might be able to see that even though he feels like sleeping in, he would have to get up if he wants lunch. However, he would not have the opportunity to learn about responsibility and consequences if he could count on his parent later to deliver his lunch to the school.

When a child says, "I'm bored," most middle class parents take that statement as an indictment of their parenting ability. There is a prevailing belief that no American child should ever know boredom or an unprogrammed or an unoccupied moment.

As long as a child says, "I'm bored," and we take responsibility for it by suggesting, "Why don't you do this, what about this?" we are teaching the child to just declare boredom and then to expect others to adapt their behavior to meet his needs.

The responsible parent, trying to develop a successful child, would handle that situation by saying, "I believe I understand a little bit about what you are feeling, son. I hope it works out," then would walk away briskly to avoid further attempts at manipulation.

We have never known a child who, if allowed to be bored for an hour, didn't become so bored with boredom that he began to exercise his native intelligence and come up with a creative menu of things to occupy his time.

Children are often able to get their parents to take responsibility for their boredom and other feelings and have them running around frantically trying to come up with ideas: "Maybe we can design a youth center. How about going to a movie? What if I buy you a new car? Could I interest you in a ski trip to Colorado?" Teaching children to hold out for the highest ante, these parents run around in terror trying to organize their children's lives. Children do not learn to be assertive and creative when parents handle all their problems for them. It works directly against genius, self-actualization, and all of the things a successful person has or does.

Parents can allow their children to experience the consequences of something small, like boredom or going without their lunch. We can allow children to experience things that won't hurt them, but will only inconvenience them, or give them a temporary bruise on their knee, or a momentary broken heart, rather than lasting, permanent damage. Then, instead of putting them down with, "Dummy, you should have realized," we can explore gently and thoughtfully, using the *what, why* and *how* (EIAG) process. "What were you feeling? What did you do in response to that feeling? Then what happened? If you want the same thing to take place next time you have that feeling, what would you do? How could you handle your anger differently if you want something else to happen?"

As soon as we can teach children to ask themselves, "What do other people do with their anger besides what I do?" they begin to generate a menu of alternatives. They will begin to think in terms of, "When I feel angry I will walk away, step outside, not go home until I've cooled off, or wait a little while before I confront anyone." They will have several alternate behaviors and will be well on their way in the development of strong intra-personal skills.

HELPING CHILDREN DEVELOP STRONG INTERPERSONAL SKILLS

One of the greatest struggles of the human race is learning how to interact with other people. The fifth of the *significant seven* helps children develop strong interpersonal skills to interact with others effectively.

INTERPERSONAL SKILLS NEEDED TO DEAL WITH OTHERS

The interpersonal skills each of us needs to work well with others are listed and defined below:

ABILITY	*DEFINITION*
Listening	Understand what is being said from the other person's point of view.
Communication	Exchange of understanding between two or more people.
Cooperation	Two or more people working together toward a common goal.
Negotiation	Give and take between two or more people to resolve conflicts.
Sharing	Including others in one's experience and activities.
Empathizing	Conveying understanding of another's feelings or needs.

DIALOGUE! DIALOGUE! DIALOGUE!

Can you guess the basis of all these transactions? If you guessed dialogue, you are right on track. Without dialogue listening is not effective, and it is difficult to communicate productively. Without effective communication it is impossible to understand individual perceptions. Without an understanding of individual perceptions there is no incentive to empathize, cooperate, negotiate, and share.

LISTENING SKILLS

The foundation of interpersonal skills is the ability to initiate and maintain a meaningful exchange of perceptions. In order to have a meaningful exchange of perceptions, we must listen actively and effectively. Listening is the most underdeveloped capability in our culture at the present time. Effective listening is the ability to form an image in our minds of what people are saying to us — to actively analyze it and check it out so that we are able in our minds to change places with another person and to see and appreciate their point of view spontaneously.

ENCOURAGING LISTENING SKILLS

In addition to the contribution of dialogue to the development of interpersonal capabilities, many other activities improve specific skills such as listening and negotiating.

The ability to listen effectively requires a special kind of training that is not being adequately cultivated in early childhood at the present time in our culture. Deficits in interpersonal skills produce inadequacies as young people move out into the world of others. This deficit tends to create a sense of impotence, hostility, and aggression for children because they don't feel in control of their relationships with others, and they don't feel understood or appreciated by the people they are working with.

We know today that dialogue and listening are also the foundation skills for reading. It is quite difficult to teach reading comprehension to an inadequate listener. After years of looking at remedial programs we have discovered that reading is less a primary skill than a product of other skills. Essentially it is a slightly different form of dialogue.

When reading, instead of forming the image of things we have heard verbally and analyzing them, we take symbols in a written form and do exactly the same thing. We must form an image in our mind of what is contained in the written message and analyze it to interpret what is involved, what it means, check it out and check the context.

The tools of the listener include learning to paraphrase accurately what people have been saying to us and learning to use "I" statements. "I" statements can sound very superficial if used as a technique, but are very effective when used occasionally with sincerity: "I am not sure I understood what you were saying; let me be sure," or "What I heard you say was _____ . "I" statements are a way of checking to be sure we understand the perceptions of others. Checking lets them know, "I do not assume that what I heard you say is what you meant. I will take the time to check."

Two active abilities are necessary in listening. One is taking what is said and comparing it with our previous experience with that individual to determine what was said. If it is consistent with what they have said to us in similar situations, it is still important to look at what might be meant by their present communication, because people do not always say what they mean. To avoid confusion or stereotyping, we need to go back and check.

There are two active tests of any message: First, we need to look at *what* this person could be saying. And secondly, we need to look at the *why* of this person's communication. We can usually program a computer to do more effective listening than many of us do with our loved ones much of the time.

When we take the time to communicate effectively and well with our children; when we avoid adultisms, instead of assuming their position; when we take the time to find out what their understanding is of the problem; we model the process of effectively working with others.

When we stop them and say, "Let me be sure I understand what you've been saying to me," we teach them to slow down and take control of the process. In doing that, we are helping them learn to think of the what?, why?, and how? by requiring it in that situation. In a way that does not frustrate them we can say, "Wait a minute. Before you tell me anything else, let me make sure I understand what you are saying to me." And we check.

NEGOTIATION

We are modeling respect for their point of view by listening, communicating, and showing them how to negotiate an understanding with people when we ask them to paraphrase back what they have heard us say: "Okay, Let me be sure you understand what I was asking you to do."

We can conduct negotiations in some situations before they are decided. We can sit down and talk with our children about what would be a reasonable time-frame to come home, for example, instead of assuming we know the only reasonable answer.

We teach negotiation when we are willing to say to a child, "I know that your activities vary, and sometimes you have to travel farther, so we will decide on a reasonable time for you to be home each time instead of setting a standard time for all occasions whereby you have to organize your life around that set time. My life doesn't work very well if I do not have any flexibility when circumstances vary. So we'll set up an agreement, but once we have agreed to a time, then that is what you will adhere to."

Flexibility allows for experience in negotiation. A willingness to be flexible also teaches young people that we respect their feelings and investments and therefore, they are learning to experience them and respect them in others. So by modeling good communication, setting up situations where we sometimes do negotiate, and opening ourselves up to an exploration and appreciation of our children's feelings, we set the stage for them to communicate, cooperate, negotiate, empathize, and share at a more effective level.

So, dialogue, the meaningful exchange of perceptions in a climate of support and interest, is the foundation ingredient for all interpersonal skills.

Skill in dialogue is also essential to moral and ethical development, critical thinking, judgmental maturity, and intellectual development. We cannot diminish the importance of parents and teachers using dialogue as the foundation for helping children develop the skills they need.

PEOPLE REDUCED TO MULTIPLE CHOICE

Parents should be aware that it is highly possible that the current methods used most widely in schools today actually increase passivity and reduce affirmation, validation, and encouragement. The effect of these methods is compounded when parents also encourage passivity by reducing kids to multiple choice and true or false answers with, "Did you? Can you? Do you? Will you? Won't you? Are you? Aren't you?" or, as they get a little older, "Why can't you ever? How come you never? Surely you realize! How many times do I have to tell you? When will you ever grow up?" These questions and statements all create a sense of threat and inadequacy in children's dealing with adults. The threat that a response would be discounted, criticized, or dismissed is a good reason not to offer one.

In an earlier chapter we gave the definition of dialogue as a meaningful exchange of perceptions in a climate of support and understanding. We can't create all these threats and then expect young people to voluntarily open up and be responsive.

IQ LEVELS RAISED

Observation of adults dealing with children consistently shows that most adults *assume* children lack the verbal skills and insight needed to answer thoughtful questions for themselves. Most adults who answer questions for children invalidate them in that process. We often make the same assumption for adolescents, and even for our spouses and others.

When working with children, adults have a tendency to anticipate their lack of skills and to reduce them to multiple choice and true and false answers: "*Did* you have a good day? *Was* that fun for you? *Do* you like this doll? *Are* you enjoying yourself?" These are close-ended questions. Open questions are "*What* feelings do you have about this? *What* kinds of things were fun for you? *What* was good about your day? *Tell* me about your favorite doll. Did you learn anything today?"

In a recent study that involved so called deprived, inner- city children, this practice on the part of adults was changed with impressive results. The researchers taught the significant adults to ask, "What things were fun for you today?" and "What did you learn?" instead of, "Did you have fun today?" and "Did you learn anything today?" They taught these adults the importance of being patient after asking open ended questions, so the children would have time to give thoughtful responses.

The researchers found that when they were able to increase the total stimulation in this area by an average of seven minutes a day, or a total of one hour per week, testable IQ rose by an average of 8 points for boys and girls between the ages 4 and 5. When these children started school, they were more confident, self-assured, and effective in responding to teachers. They showed higher bonding of closeness and trust and involvement with those adults who were significant in their lives. Dialogue is a very powerful strategy for affirming, validating, and encouraging people.

DEVELOPMENTAL LEVELS

Adults need to be aware of the developmental levels of children. Children's perceptual abilities change as they grow and develop physically, mentally, and emotionally.

Very often our expectations of people are beyond what they are capable of at the time. Expectations that are too high are threatening to children. On the other hand, not expecting children to use the abilities they have is extremely discouraging to children.

Often we are not aware of how our interactions with children help program their initial *floppy disc* about who they are. If we are always saying, "Don't do that, you are too little, never try to get something without checking with me," we are saying, "I have absolutely no confidence in or for your ability to do things for yourself." This lack of confidence will create a dependent person who is put in a double bind when we later criticize him for not taking more responsibility.

From ages zero to five, children learn a great deal about themselves as a result of how we deal with them. Then at about five they begin to act on what they believe about themselves. Rather than allowing them to continue to develop clarity in a familiar environment, we send them off to school in strange surroundings. Over the next two or three years, with no basic experience to draw from, they are quite vulnerable to how we interact with them in the school setting.

If they run into rather closed, judgmental people, who frequently discount what they think or believe, they will learn to be quite passive and tentative in offering anything. If they run into affirming people, who know how to encourage them to explore ideas and think, then they will become increasingly confident, assertive, and skilled in interacting with others.

COMPLICATIONS OF PUBERTY IN THE DEVELOPMENTAL PROCESS

Through whatever happens over the first seven or eight years, children accumulate input about themselves and just begin to pull it together as they approach 9 or 10 years old. All of us who have dealt with children in this age range find they are delightfully clear in their perceptions of the world. They take all their experiences and perceptions and begin to reach conclusions and develop fairly consistent patterns. They show that false window of clarity where they feel quite certain in their knowledge of what life is all about. "We are Presbyterians. They are Catholics. We don't eat pizza. We don't have those kinds of friends. We don't watch those kinds of shows."

HERE COME THE HORMONES

Just when they get a grip on life and begin to act with some sense of awareness, what happens? Massive doses of testosterone and progesterone come roaring through their bodies and wipe out everything. They must essentially start all over to discover a new person. A whole new *floppy disk* pops out of their *computer* with no programs on it, called new body, new moods, new feelings, new impulses. When we watch them, we will see that any group of 12 year olds have a six year gap, in either direction, between their minds and their bodies.

In one family the firstborn daughter had an 18 year old physical plant with an 11 year old board of trustees directing her around town. Right behind her came another daughter at age 15, who was intellectually precocious, with a 20 year old level mind trapped in an 11 year old, prepubescent body without a curve or hair anywhere in sight. One would look down at her body and say, "Will this ever stop?" The other one, looking in the same direction would say, "Will anything ever start?" These concerns can be very distracting for adolescents who have so many new things happening all at once.

By the age of thirteen life has become very immediate and turbulent. For 13-year-olds, a long term goal is frequently three hours. A life's dream is frequently a week. They can seem very close to hopeless ecstacy one minute, and a zit will show up and throw them into terminal depression right on the spot. "I'll die if this big dipper is still here on Saturday!!!

JUDGEMENT AND THREAT

During this time, parents have found a way to be very discouraging. Seeing the new bumps and hairs, and recognizing the potential implications, they step in anxiously and intensify the problem with, "Why can't you ever? How come you never? Surely you realize! How many times do I have to tell you? When will you ever grow up? You knew better than that! You are too big to behave this way."

In essence, these adultisms imply to young people, "I have been accumulating data on your inadequacies for years, so this doesn't surprise me at all. In addition to everything else that you are trying to get a grip on, there is a large shopping list of ideas and expectations you don't comprehend, so you must be in worse shape than you think."

Can't you just imagine a child, after hearing all this dumped on them, saying, "Dad, there are a couple of other inadequacies you overlooked that I need some help with." Instead, he will be thinking, "You are the last person on Earth that I can go near in honesty because I want you to think well of me, but I am rapidly using up all my credit with you."

LYING AND DISTORTING

Perceived threat produces a sense of powerlessness and despair. Adultisms create conditions in which children who want us to love and accept them begin to lie and misrepresent to save what is left of our good opinion of them. Very frequently parents fail to understand that children who lie and misrepresent things, who try to make themselves look better, are usually doing so because they want their parents to think well of them.

Parents often misinterpret the purposes behind lying, punish them harder, and become more judgmental and hostile. We forget that children base their behavior on what they *perceive is true*, not on their parent's perceptions of what is true. By forgetting to see things from children's perceptions we drive them deeper and deeper into irrational behavior in their effort to be independent and still keep our love. We create a threatening environment rather than an environment of support where effective communication, cooperation, negotiation and problem-solving can make practical change take place.

WHY LYING AND MISREPRESENTATION CAN MAKE SENSE

Adultisms are a primary source of threat leading to dishonesty, avoidance, and denial. Children around the age of six to eight often lie when they are anxious to prove their independence yet still want the love and security of their parents. They often think they will find their independence by doing what they want yet still keep the approval of their parents by covering their attempts at independence by lying.

Lying and misrepresentation becomes prevalent again with the onset of puberty when children, who are insecure about their identity, are well aware that they are not living up to many of the expectations of adults and are also sorting through a new body, new emotions, and new feelings. Adultisms are a grossly unnecessary complication which will drive them into the arms of their peer group, increase their tendency to avoid contact with adults, and become defensive in their transactions with adults. Adultisms are very expensive.

DEPARTMENT STORE SEMINAR

When I was in a department store the other day, seeing how my neighbor's shop and doing research for my workshops, I saw a mini seminar in human relationships. A mother rushed up to her child and demanded, "How many times do I have to tell you not to touch the toys?"

The child answered, "Eleven!"

The mother lost it right there, "What do you mean, eleven?"

The child said, "I don't know."

She was safe again because "I don't know" is often the only safe answer. This child quickly learned that the last thing on Earth her parent wanted was a thoughtful response. What her mother really wanted was to make her feel dumb, inadequate, and childish.

I left the toy department and approached the checkout stand where I saw a more advanced seminar in relationships. There was a 13-year-old who had obviously started puberty but hadn't gone anywhere with it. As I got there, the parent said, "Why are you angry?"

I wanted to drop to my knees and give him an honest answer. "Because a frontal system passing through has upset the pressure gradient in ways that are producing subtle changes in my limbic system. That, together with the over-abundance of highly processed starch, sugar, fats, and carbohydrates that they saturated me with at the lunch line because they were cheap, along with the overwhelming frustration of trying to contain all those ambient calories without moving, wiggling, or fidgeting through the next three hours of required classes, with only four minutes to get to the bathroom and the next class, created a lot of pent up energy and frustration that I carried onto the school bus where they said, 'Sit down. Shut up. Close the window. Pipe down. I'm going to tell your parents. You are going to get a suspension for this;' I then stepped off the bus with all that going on and added a dose of caffeine and sugar from a Pepsi plus theobromine from a brownie, which went roaring up through the inherited instability of my hypothalamus from three generations of alcoholics in my pedigree, not to mention the normal instability due to puberty. All of this turbulence then bounced off a massive dose of testosterone roaring through me to get me ready for puberty, which greatly magnified the frustration of trying to meet and anticipate adult expectations all day so that it was just more than I could handle."

That statement, of course, is a little difficult for a 13- year-old to try to articulate, so what this one said was, "Because!"

The parent said, "What do you mean, 'because?'"

And the kid said, "I don't know," because that was the only reply that was safe.

NO PANTS

As I approached my home, I heard a graduate seminar going on at my neighbor's house. He messes up a lot with his window open, so I have a lot of neat things for my workshops. As I was coming down the driveway, I heard from his house, "Where are my brown pants? You knew I would need them for my next trip. Every week, it's the same thing. Nothing is ready. I can't earn a living naked."

Now compare that with, "Honey, what was your understanding of what I planned to take with me on this trip?"

"Well, to tell the truth we never discussed it."

"Ah, that could explain why my brown pants aren't here."

"As far as I know you never took them to the cleaners, did you?"

"I thought you were going to do that."

"Well, dear, you've been so fussy about your pants for the last few weeks, I just knew you would want to handle that yourself. I'll tell you what. If it's real important to you, I'll try to drop them off this week, and they will be here for your next trip."

In either case, he has no brown pants! But if he continues with the first method, he soon has no wife, no children, and no closet to put his pants in. He has alimony, child support, an efficiency apartment, and a therapist.

Which of these examples shows love, caring, dignity and respect? Which one shows hostility, aggression, lack of caring, and disrespect?

INSTANT REPLAY

Let's go back to the department store. The mother could have said to the four-year-old, "Honey, what was your understanding of what I asked you to do with the toys?" Soon she would have a child who would often wait and deal with her rather than a child who ran around the store trying to second guess her.

The parent could have said to the adolescent by the check out stand, "I can see you are very upset son," instead of requiring him to be articulate about feelings he never had before. "When you settle down, I would like to go over it with you to make sure I understand what caused the problem."

The latter response is respectful and shows recognition of the young person's struggle. It would convey empathy without requiring him to be articulate at a time when he is struggling for control and understanding of himself. This response is not demeaning. It allows him to preserve his dignity, yet conveys interest and concern. It also models communication, empathy, good listening, and other interpersonal skills and encourages their development in others.

"You keep a civil tongue in your head. I don't know why you would be upset," is a response that does not allow for any of the above.

BARRIERS TO THE DEVELOPMENT OF INTERPERSONAL SKILLS

1. *Lack of Respect for Unique Perceptions*

One of the greatest barriers is the lack of respect for the unique perceptions of others. When we travel to another country, we do not get along very well if we spend our time criticizing the way they do things in other cultures. We broaden our knowledge and experience when we make every effort to understand, respect, and enjoy different cultures.

In a way, each individual is a different culture. When we remember this and approach each individual with interest, respect, and a desire to learn about his or her unique way of viewing the world, we eliminate most of the conflict and frustration experienced in relationships.

2. *The Big Five*

The five barriers discussed in Chapter Four are also counterproductive to the development of interpersonal skills. So by removing those five barriers and then developing a language that promotes dialogue to replace the barriers of, "Did you? Can you? Do you? Will you?" not only will young people feel more capable around us, but they are more likely to be responsive to us when we want to talk with them and, therefore, begin to develop strong interpersonal skills.

3. *Television*

Another barrier is television. The more time children spend with television, the less skilled they become in dialogue. In early childhood this lack of practice in dialogue is particularly lethal.

Most authorities recommend no more than six hours a week of exposure to television in a child's first six years of life. Any more time has to be deducted from the amount of time a child spends actively and personally formulating images, exchanging ideas, asserting themselves in the environment, and interacting with significant others. Those are primary activities for this age group. It is how they begin to develop all their foundation capabilities.

4. *Lack of Dialogue in Families*

We keep emphasizing the importance of dialogue, which was one of the factors lost during families in transition. Dialogue was once the primary center of family life; even if children weren't talking a great deal, their most interesting activity most of the time was to hear the thoughts, expressions, ideas, reactions, and interchanges between real people (as opposed to television characters) they were trying to identify with, understand, and be like.

Today children have *Baretta, Kojak, Dukes of Hazzard, Charlie's Angels, The Incredible Hulk, General Hospital, Dallas, Dynasty* and *Home Box Office* instead of dialogue with parents. And we wonder where they get all their bizarre ideas.

BRINGING DIALOGUE BACK

If we want to affirm, validate, and lay a foundation of interpersonal skills in children, we have to substitute the "did you, can you, do you, will you, won't you, are you, aren't you," which is the language of disrespect, and use the language of respect, which is "what, where, when, how, in what way, and under what circumstances, let me be sure I understand, what was your understanding of."

One of the ways we train young people to develop strong interpersonal skills is to explore through dialogue, the what, the why, and the how of their experiences.

Instead of focusing on the experiences when children did things capably for themselves or were an important, contributing part of something or had some power to influence things, we are now focusing on analyzing, interpreting, and understanding other people's perceptions, feelings, and point-of-view.

SOME KEYS TO SUCCESS

1. *Practice* respectful dialogue in your own life.

2. *Model* empathy, listening, and negotiation for children as you deal with them.

3. *Structure* as many situations as possible to require practice in one or more of these skills and then be patient and acknowledge successful and unsuccessful efforts.

With enough experience young people will be able to use their interpersonal skills spontaneously when they must resolve differences, work with others, understand the feelings of others, and deal effectively with their own ideas, feelings, and needs.

Chapter 9

HELPING CHILDREN DEVELOP STRONG SYSTEMIC SKILLS

The sixth of the *significant seven* helps people develop the skills necessary to recognize and deal with relationships in their environment. These skills include responsibility, adaptability, and flexibility.

SYSTEMIC SKILLS

Systems consist of things that are directly related such as cause and effect, limits and consequences, privileges and responsibilities, principles of organization, and principles of physics. All of these concepts exist only in a context of relationships, or how elements fit together or interact with each other.

CAUSE AND EFFECT

Children need to understand cause and effect and limits. An understanding of cause and effect that is reasonable and appropriate can lead to acceptance of the inevitable. When children have strong systemic skills and can recognize limits, they will know when to accept those limits and when to think of creative ways to work around or within those limits.

These skills are primary to areas of leadership, super productivity, and to the area we call genius. Genius is very often the ability to see an alternate relationship between finite or infinite things in the universe.

GOAL SETTING

Setting and achieving goals is possible when children have strong systemic skills. Setting a goal requires an understanding of what outcome is desired, what relationships must be dealt with, and what steps must be taken to orchestrate those relationships to achieve the goal. The core of systemic skills is responsibility.

RESPONSIBILITY

Responsibility has been described as the ability to recognize and act appropriately upon the principles of relatedness in the environment. A responsible person is one who perceives the interaction of elements and principles in their world and is able to work with them effectively.

ADAPTABILITY

Adaptability is one of the strongest survival capabilities of the human race and is a concept that has been overlooked in an age of specialization and increasing pre-occupation with finding the *real me*.

In the height of the *me* generation the notion was conveyed that everybody was on a search through life looking for the *real me*, as if somewhere out there in space was this constantly valid identity called *myself*. In reality, human beings exist as a multiplicity of selves. They are as multifaceted as the world's largest diamond. Each facet of a person is valid in a given context and invalid in other contexts. The sooner we learn that, the closer we come to maturity.

Maturity is that point in life when each of us learns to creatively manage our own multiplicity. We have learned the skill of adaptability when we creatively use the facet of our personality that is appropriate at the time. Immature people erroneously believe they have only one facet to their personality which they apply to all situations. They ignore feedback, fail to anticipate consequences of their behavior, and never learn how to effectively adapt without unnecessarily compromising. A typical comment made by these people is, "That is just the way I am."

A TIME AND A PLACE FOR EVERYTHING

At this moment I exist in many forms: husband, friend, counselor, coach, lover, child and many more. Each is legitimately me. Each is appropriate in one context and inappropriate in another.

Suppose I have been away on a trip. All week I have been lecturer, counselor, consultant, psychologist. Even though I have gaged my funds closely, I arrive home in the evening close to bankruptcy. I discover I have just enough, if I shake my pockets, to pay the ransom on my car and head for home. The airline food wasn't that good, so I am still hungry. On the way home I pass the golden arches and have a *Big Mac* attack but do not have enough money with which to respond. It is approaching the end of the month. I have all the billing from my trip and many other bills to pay. By the time I reach home, the accountant facet of my personality is ruminating over all of the financial challenges I face.

When I arrive home, it is late in the evening. As I approach the door and reach out for it, it opens. I see on the wall the flickering of candles. I hear the easy listening station that I like best. As I am about to step into the doorway, a lovely person, in an obviously new negligee, steps out from behind the door to greet me.

At that exact moment, if the accountant is standing there, I am in deep difficulty because I would say, "How much did that cost? What's the matter, did they cut off the electricity?" The repercussions of that kind of response at that time could echo throughout the relationship for years.

If I am a mature person, I would read the situation and ask what outcome do I most desire at this moment? If I desire to put my wife down and grumpily strut my stuff as an accountant, I could do that. On the other hand, if I realize that she has obviously gone to a great deal of difficulty to let me know that it was not the accountant that was most missed this trip, I can look at what other aspects of myself would be more appropriate to this situation. An obvious choice would be to say to the accountant, "Get lost for awhile," and pull out lover, friend, responder, and warm human being and apply that response to the situation.

I have a choice. I can adapt successfully to that situation to both affirm another person, validate what I want most out of that moment, and have a mellow time with candles and music. Or, I can chose the *pseudo* real me and respond with, "Hey, don't give me this crap. I'm broke." This would be an inappropriate and irresponsible choice which would hurt another person and destroy closeness and intimacy in the relationship.

Suppose the next weekend, in anticipation of repeating another romantic welcome, I find myself running through the airport, leaping the turnstile, leaving my bag behind to be claimed on another day, ignoring the golden arches, whipping home ready for love and come down the driveway, leave my briefcase in the car, and race toward the door, which doesn't open by itself. Once I finally get my key out and unlock it, the lights are all going brightly. As I come into the room, my potential friend and lover is down on her knees, in jeans, scrubbing up a mess left by a sick child. In that moment if I

151

choose to go over and pat her on the backside and say, "Hey, I'm ready for love," I probably would be wearing the towel she is using on my head. This obviously is the moment to say to the lover, "You had better get lost for awhile." At this time it is more appropriate to become a helpmate and friend and say, "Wow honey, it looks like you have had a hell of a night. What can I do to help you out?" That response would indicate a mature ability to consider a situation and adapt effectively to it. Many young people have a very limited repertoire of options and have not learned to adapt, so they apply inappropriate aspects of themselves to situations and endlessly complicate their lives.

FLEXIBILITY

The palm tree has flexibility so that it can bend with the wind. When it bends with the wind, does it remain laid over? No. It has learned to bend with a wind that is strong enough to tear its roots out if it remained rigid. When the wind is gone, it can straighten itself up again.

Flexibility is learning not to be so rigid that we are broken by encounters and locked into an unworkable position. The ultimate definition of insanity is to inflexibly do the same thing over and over while hoping for a different outcome.

TWO PRIMARY BARRIERS

Both strictness and permissiveness, as outlined in Chapter Six, discourage the development of systemic skills and should be avoided.

1. *Strictness*

Strictness is the excessive imposition of power which usually involves some type of punishment. When strictness is used, the adult maintains all control and responsibility while the child learns to comply or to rebel rather than think and respond.

In the next chapter on self-discipline, responsibility, and judgement we point out that one of the common errors of control based on reward and punishment is that it limits people to a pre-conventional level of human understanding. In other words, it keeps them at a level of stimulus/response of either obeying or rebelling.

An understanding of the developmental process can help us understand why spanking, although hardly ever the most effective teaching tool, can seem effective for children between the ages of two to six. They are then at the stimulus/response level and don't *think* about the spanking so much as they *respond*. However, when children mature into perceptual human beings, they begin to *think* about punishment after their initial reaction. The results of their thinking are usually manifested in one of two extremes: rebellion or low self-esteem.

The following *Three R's of Punishment* outlines the range of thinking most young people follow after punishment:

THE THREE R'S OF PUNISHMENT

1. **Resentment:** "This is unfair. I can't trust adults."

2. **Revenge:** "They are winning now, but I'll get even."

3. **Retreat** in one of three extremes:

   a. **Rebellion:** "I'll do what I want and just be more careful not to get caught next time. I have a right to lie and cheat under these circumstances."

   b. **Reduced self-esteem:** "I must really be a bad person who deserves to be punished. I will keep trying to please, but I'm not much good at it."

   c. **Retirement:** "I give up. I can't win, so why try? I wish people would just leave me alone."

Many adults gain a false perception of punishment because it *seems* to work: it usually stops the misbehavior for the immediate moment. However, when we take a look at the long-range results described in the Three R's of Punishment we obviously need to use more effective means to teach children the relationship between what they do and the results they obtain.

2. *Permissiveness*

Permissiveness does not create an environment in which consequences are experienced. Both parent and child abdicate responsibility. Children learn to use their energy and intelligence to manipulate others into rescuing and protecting them from the consequences and results of their behavior. The long-range results are devastating when children find that they cannot manipulate other people the way they did their parents. Their *rude awakening* often results in a life of frustration, anger, or depression.

Parents are often permissive because it is *easier.* The long-range results are devastating when parents find that taking care of their children's needs is not easy as they get older and more demanding; and it is not easy to bail them out of the problems they create when they believe *the world owes them a living.*

THE PRIMARY BUILDERS

There are three essential elements of teaching responsibility and the other systemic skills:

1. *Unqualified positive regard, love, and/or respect.* Unqualified positive regard is possible only when we remember some of the things we have already discussed, like understanding and respecting differences in perceptions, learning styles, and developmental levels.

2. *Clear feedback about behavior.* We need to give recognition and appreciation for acceptable behavior and accomplishment and avoid generic praise. And, we need to give specific feedback for unacceptable behavior and avoid generic criticism.

3. *A consequential environment.* We create a consequential environment when we follow up with firmness, dignity, and respect decisions that have been agreed upon. The use of natural and logical consequences is an excellent way to provide children with the opportunity to develop systemic skills.

NATURAL AND LOGICAL CONSEQUENCES

One of the best ways to teach young people that they have control over their environment is to let them experience direct consequences of their actions, then through the *What?, Why? and How?* process, help them see how they can achieve different consequences through different behavior.

NATURAL CONSEQUENCES

Natural consequences are what happen *naturally* as the result of certain choices or behaviors. For example, when we go out in the rain without a raincoat, we get wet. If we forget to take a lunch, we go hungry. Children could learn so much if we would allow them to experience natural consequences without adult interference.

If a child loses her baseball mitt, the natural consequence would be for her to live without a baseball mitt. She would learn a lot from that experience. However, most parents cannot stand for their little darlings to do without, especially if it would mean missing a Little League game. That attitude would be fine if these parents would tell the truth and simply say, "I can't stand it for you to miss the game, so you don't have to be responsible. Anytime you lose your mitt, I will rush out and buy you a new one.

Instead, the conversation goes more like this: "How many times have I told you to take care of your mitt? If you would be more responsible, this would not happen. When will you ever learn?" The lecture continues all the time this parent is out *helping* the child look for her mitt.

The ultimate lie is usually told on the way to the store to buy a new mitt: "This is absolutely the last time I will buy you a new mitt if you lose this one." They both know it is not the last time.

Instead, the child would learn quickly from a parent who would be firm with dignity and respect: "Gee, honey, I'm sorry you lost your mitt. That must be very disappointing," and leave it at that no matter how much the child begs and cries for a new one. That would be a natural consequence. Children are much less likely to be irresponsible when they have to experience the consequences of their own behavior.

For parents who truly cannot stand to have their child miss the Little League game, the next best alternative would be to impose a logical consequence.

GUIDELINES FOR NATURAL CONSEQUENCES

Natural consequences should not be used under the following circumstances:

1. *When there is immediate danger to the child.* A child should not be allowed to experience the natural consequence of running into the street.

2. *When there is immediate danger to another person or property.* A child should not be allowed to experience the natural consequences of throwing a rock at someone or through a window. In both of these cases is it best, as Rudolph Dreikurs put

it, "to shut your mouth and act." Teaching can come later when a climate of support has been established.

3. *When future consequences are at stake.* A child should not be allowed to experience the natural consequences of not brushing his/her teeth or of poor eating habits.

4. *When a child is not old enough to understand the responsibility involved in preventing the natural consequence.* A two-year old cannot be expected to remember his or her lunch for pre-school.

5. *When adults cannot "keep their mouths shut. "* The benefits of a natural consequence are voided when adults add their comments. If a child is going hungry as a natural consequence of forgetting her lunch, she will likely be thinking about how to avoid this experience in the future and could be learning internal locus of control. If an adult intervenes with, "That is what you get for being irresponsible. How many times do I have to remind you? Maybe next time you will remember," the child's attention is more likely focused on the *mean old adult*, and could be developing a belief in external locus of control.

WHAT?, WHY?, HOW?

After a cooling off period, natural consequences should be followed with the EIAG process to check on the conclusions that young people have reached as a result of their experience and to help them arrive at different conclusions when appropriate.

LOGICAL CONSEQUENCES

Logical consequences do not happen naturally; they are set up by adults or by children. In this case it might sound like "I'll be happy to take you to the store to buy a new mitt if you have saved enough money from your allowance to pay for it, or if you would like to have the money deducted from your allowance. However, I have a very busy schedule today and going to the store will take about half and hour. As soon as you have helped me accomplish one of my chores, we will leave. Would you like to weed for half an hour or wash my car?" Giving in to promises from the child to complete the chore later is an invitation for a power struggle later to get it done.

Many parents have asked, "Well, if my child knows in advance that he is going to get a spanking, isn't that a logical consequence?"

It is not. A consequence is not logical if it is lacking in any of the following Three R's of Logical Consequences:

THREE R'S OF LOGICAL CONSEQUENCES

1. RELATED to the behavior

2. RESPECTFUL to both child and adult

3. REASONABLE to both child and adult

A spanking is not logically related to any behavior. Spanking is not respectful — it is hurtful and humiliating. And, although there are many adults who think it is reasonable, you won't find many children who believe spanking is reasonable. There was a time in our developmental level as a species that spanking was effective. However, the more intelligent we become in our developmental progress as a species, the less effective it becomes.

The next question is usually, "Then what about the next two popular methods for discipline today: grounding and removal of privileges? Are they logical consequences?"

The answer is, "Yes and no."

WHAT IS NOT AS IMPORTANT AS WHY AND HOW

We must keep in mind that it is not what we do so much As why we are doing it and how we are doing it. The why has to do with the results we would like to achieve. The how has to do with our attitude and tone of voice. Actually, the why will usually determine the how.

Grounding is usually not effective for positive long-range results when adults use it for revenge, to make children suffer, or to show them who is boss or because we don't know what else to do. Grounding can be effective for positive long-range results when it is related to the misbehavior, is done in a respectful manner, and is reasonable. Reasonable is often determined by the way the logical consequence was set up in the first place. Logical consequences can be reasonable by agreement when they are set up in advance by adults and children together when they are not caught up in the emotions of conflict.

Grounding that is ineffective might sound like this: "I don't want to hear your excuses. Get to your room and think about the terrible thing you did. I don't understand how you could have done such a thing. I can't tell you how disappointed I am in you." The reason for the grounding in this case is more to put the child down than to inspire him to do better.

Grounding that is effective might sound like this: "We all make mistakes. Go to your room until you feel better, then we will work on a solution." The reason for the grounding in this case is to create a *cooling off period* until a climate of support can be created in which to work on improvement in small steps.

ADVANCE PREPARATION

It is a good idea to discuss the purpose of grounding with children in advance. Let them know that the purpose is not to humiliate them, punish them, or make them suffer. The purpose is to give everyone involved a chance to calm down. When the purpose is to calm down, it is valid to suggest that while they are in their room, they might want to read, listen to music, take a nap, or play with some games.

Some adults see this as rewarding negative behavior. These adults mistakenly believe that children will not *do better* until after they *feel worse*. Making children feel *worse* creates a threatening environment in which constructive learning does not take place. Making them feel better and leaving it at that is not recommended either. The point is to create a climate of support and then to work on constructive learning.

After children have experienced a consequence that follows the Three R's of Logical Consequences, even if they didn't like it at the time, they are usually left with a feeling of fairness and self-responsibility. However, when they experience punishment, even though it seems to stop the behavior at the time, they are usually left with negative feelings described in the Three R's of Punishment.

CHILD HOME LATE

What usually happens when a child is due home at 12:00? 12:30 comes, no child. What do most parents do in the absence of data? They immediately assume the worst — raped, killed, run off, missing, eloped, accident. By 1:30 we are on a peak of fear, adrenalin, and anxiety. Then they show up suddenly, having survived our worst fears, and we are livid with them for their survival. What prompted all that concern? Love. Is that what we gave them when they got home?

A Mature parent would say, "Son, I'm glad you are home. I was beginning to think of the terrible things that might have happened, and I got in touch with how much I love you. We will talk in the morning about what this will mean for the rest of the month."

Now what do young people do in the absence of data? They assume the worst — grounded forever, no prom, no car. By 5:00 a.m. they will be in our bedrooms, "Is it morning yet, Dad?"

"No, still sleeping in here." They'll be back at 7:00, "Are you ready yet?"

"No, I'm sleeping in this morning."

COOLING OFF PERIOD

Mature parents refuse to deal with the most important people in their life when they are at their worst. Coming of the peak of fear, adrenalin, and anxiety is no time to do anything but make an idiot of ourselves.

My daughter was once asked, "What is the hardest thing about dealing with your dad?"

She said, "When I make a mistake, he is quiet, and he respects me. That way I know it is my problem. It was so much nicer when he used to yell and scream and make an ass out of himself. Then I knew it was his problem."

Whenever children sense our anger coming toward them, they believe it is our anger, and not what they did that, is causing problems for them. So if we can keep our dignity and give them theirs, we come out in good shape.

CONSIDER THE AGE

Age is an important consideration in determining logical consequences. Logical consequences for children of age birth to three years old should not last longer that 5 to 10 minutes. One hour is a long time for three to six year old children. Consequences for children six to eight years of age should not last longer than one day. From 8 to 12 a week is plenty, and for ages 12 through 18 consequences should not exceed one month.

Consequences that last over a 24 period for a child up to 8, over a week for a child up to 12, and over a month for a child up to 17, are like consecutive life sentences. Consequences that last too long for the age level do nothing to solve a problem and destroy any incentive to try. We want to squeeze them enough to get their attention but have it over soon enough to inspire them to do better if we want positive change. Anything beyond that is punishment to get even, and they will get even with us by not growing and by learning to dodge us along the way.

The extremes of not being aware of child readiness was demonstrated by two neighbors. One neighbor used the belt in anger on his five-year-old. The child could not possibly be thinking about anything except the pain of that beating and afterwards would most likely feel bewildered or angry.

The other neighbor said to his five-year-old, "Honey, given the existential reality of our relationship and our need to be mellow and affirming together, I mean, like if it wouldn't bum you out too much " and that child was totally bewildered. That is way too much rhetoric for a five-year-old.

A five-year-old can understand, "Honey, it is a rule in our family that we don't take plates of food into the family room. From now on you will need to eat at the table."

Then, if the child takes food into the family room, it is not effective to say, "How many times do I have to tell you?" Effective follow-up would be, "Honey, what is our rule?" After about 30 or 40 times a five-year-old will begin to understand.

Then they will see you heading for the family room with food and will say, "It is a rule in this family that we don't take food into the family room." They can reach such clarity during this age.

Children will work at such a level until about seven or eight years of age when they begin to ask questions like, "Why is that a rule in this family?"

This is not the time to say, "Because I said so." They are not testing you. They are trying to substitute conditioned behavior for insight and understanding. They are trying to make the jump to conventional reasoning.

A wise parent would respond, "Honey, I made that rule when you were little because we had some nice furniture in the family room, and I was trying to protect it. Now, what rules can you think of to help me protect what we have left?"

By running through the process of getting them involved at this time, they will generally come up with some rules because they will feel it is a vote of confidence from you that they are getting older and can do and understand more of what you do and understand.

When they reach eleven, it is not appropriate to say, "Hey, if you are going to hassle me, stay out as long as you want. We will see you around over the weekend." This is way too much latitude.

At this age they can understand, "Under normal circumstances you should plan on 10:30 for your curfew. That doesn't mean you can't ever do anything after that time, but it means you shouldn't plan on it. Come and talk with me if there is something special, and I will consider it."

By the age of 17 we should be avoiding statements like, "You know your curfew is always 11:00 p.m. We already discussed this three years ago." We are then likely to have a kids driving 100 miles an hour around town the night it is their turn to drop everybody off, so they can make it under the wire. Those same kids, if they don't get killed trying to make it under unreasonable circumstances, will later go away to college or work and possible self-destruct with all that freedom they have never learned to handle with judgement. The family will think it was college that destroyed them, when in reality it was the parents' failure to anticipate that with that driver's license came a need for increased freedom and more flexibility in terms of scheduling along with increased responsibility and self-discipline.

By seventeen it is more appropriate to say, "We need to go over what you plan to do so we can arrive at a reasonable time to expect you home. Once the limit is set, your responsibility is to respect our decision if you want the privilege. By keeping our agreed upon commitments, you demonstrate that you are responsible enough to supervise yourself."

NON-VERBAL CONSEQUENCES

Logical consequences do not have to be verbal and can start at a very young age. When a toddler touches the television knobs, she can be put into a playpen without a word or cross look. In five minutes she can be taken out of the playpen. As soon as she touches the television she can be put back into the playpen. It does not take too long for very young children to make the connection that if they do not want to be in the playpen they had better stay away from the television.

GET CHILDREN INVOLVED

Whenever possible have young people join in the logical consequence process. They grasp the Three R's of Logical Consequences very quickly from the age of four years old. An excellent time to work on logical consequences is during family meetings.

Once an agreement has been reached, get the terms clear while there is an atmosphere of cooperation. Don't say, "If you don't do it, you will suffer." Be clear on exactly what the suffering will be and for how long and under what circumstances.

SEAL THE DISCUSSION WITH DIALOGUE

After setting a limit, avoid saying, "Do you understand?" Use dialogue to clarify the agreement: "What is your understanding of what will happen if you don't pick up your toys?"

As children get older they are capable of understanding the relationship of a longer sequence of events: "What is your understanding of what time you must be home? What is your understanding of what will happen if you are not home at that time? Who then will decide whether you continue to go out? How will you make that decision tonight?"

FIRMNESS

When follow-through is required, it is important to be firm. We need to live up to what we have led our children to expect. We can love them enough to say what we mean and to mean what we say and be willing to run the risk of children's temporary displeasure in order to confirm our love and respect for them with firm follow-through.

Research shows that children whose parents won't set reasonable limits or who won't follow through on the ones that have been set, believe that their parents do not love them. Children whose parents are too strict or arbitrary have the same problem because dignity and respect are compromised in most cases.

DIGNITY

Dignity means following through on agreements without projecting anger at the child. Human beings go through a strange metamorphosis when they feel anger directed toward them. They believe that their problems are due to the anger rather than their actions. The drunk who comes home to a wife who reads him the riot act in anger goes to bed very secure saying, "No wonder I drink with an unreasonable old bag like that waiting for me at home."

RESPECT

Respect is demonstrated primarily through our attitude and tone of voice. Respect begins with the belief that children create their own difficulties without additional help from us. Once we have placed privileges and responsibilities in their hands, we need to respect what they do with them and avoid doing something to get even with them because we are unhappy or feel powerless over what has happened.

Respect is, "Son, I am sorry you decided to handle it this way, but I have to respect the decision you just made to cancel your plans for the rest of the month."

When we take something from children to punish them for what they did, that is seen as unrelated and unfair and will create more resistance.

MANIPULATION

Young people may try to manipulate, "But Dad, there was this seven foot caterpillar crawling across the interstate, all the phone booths were filled with winos and derelicts." When it is clearly manipulation and we see it as *off the wall*, we can step back quickly and let it hit the other wall without getting involved. It is absolutely incredible that a grown person will stand around at 1:00 o'clock in the morning lobbying for his/her position when it is the kid's position that is untenable.

It is important to consider possible extenuating circumstances fairly; however, we should not accept or get involved in excuses that are unreasonable, invalid, or unsound.

When we must get involved, we can just clarify with *what?, why? and how?* questions to understand the child's perception of the events and then make the best judgement we can. For example, "Son, I believe I understand what took place. However, I don't believe that it was sufficient to prevent you from calling me to let me know, or at least to make other arrangements to get home on time, so I must hold you to the original agreement and ask you to cancel your plans for the next three weeks."

When a child who is expected home at 12:30 but calls at 11:45 or 12:00 to request a change, we can usually try to accommodate it since the child respected us enough to call in time for us to say no and still be home on time. When the same child calls at 12:45, get him/her home the best way possible and normally do not consider the request since the decision was likely already made when the call came.

SUMMARY

Since the teaching of responsibility produces such challenges and pressures for most families, we will summarize the steps.

1. *Avoid strictness* (excessive control for the age and maturity of the child.)

2. *Avoid permissiveness* (excessive autonomy, too little structure and follow-through for the age and maturity of the child.)

3. *Convey unqualified love/care/respect* (keep what is done separate from what people are and avoid using love, praise and approval as a reward.)

4. *Give clear feedback* (I feel _____ about _____ because_____) about behavior.

5. *Structure consequences* (connect cause and effect, privileges and responsibilities in the child's mind.)

6. *Be firm* (say what you mean and mean what you say.)

7. *Maintain dignity* (avoid projecting anger or other feelings onto the child. Be an actor rather than a re-actor. Choose to deal with things when you are at your best rather than at your worst.)

8. *Teach with respect* (clarify what they have caused to happen rather than what you have done to punish them.)

Successful application of these principles promotes responsibility, adaptability, and flexibility. It also contributes to maturity in judgement which we will explore in the next chapter.

Chapter 10

HELPING CHILDREN DEVELOP STRONG JUDGMENTAL SKILLS

The seventh of the *significant seven* helps children develop strong judgmental skills so they have the ability to analyze a situation and make accurate decisions in terms of whether it is safe-dangerous, fair-unfair, appropriate-inappropriate, moral-immoral, or ethical-unethical. Judgement requires taking an abstract idea and applying it to real life.

TRAINING IS NECESSARY

Tragically, many parents believe that judgement is like sex: children should be born with it, but not practice it for a long, long time!

Unfortunately, there is only one way to develop judgmental skills and that is to practice. Each person must serve an apprenticeship with those more mature than he or she is in order to develop this capability.

BARRIERS TO THE DEVELOPMENT OF JUDGEMENT:

1. *Unaware Parents*

Parents find it easier and more expedient to lecture, instruct, explain, moralize, make all the judgments, and tell kids what to do instead of creatively engage them in thinking through an issue or an event.

Adults who lecture, instruct, explain, and/or moralize, actually retard judgmental maturity, retard the acquisition of wisdom, retard critical thinking, and generally produce threat and intimidation.

2. *Naive Peers*

Peers are often the primary vehicle for learning and experience. Judgmental development is retarded when peers are the main source of information because peer means same level of insight, awareness, and understanding. When peers have dialogue primarily with peers, they replicate the same level of insight and naivety.

In the traditional family, interaction with siblings was important to the developmental process, as was time spent with grandparents and working alongside parents.

In the world we came from, children spent very little time with peers. Almost all of their time was spent with siblings or extended family. They spent more time with older members of the family than they did with any group of kids their own age who were not related to the same family system.

Today kids spend more time in peer centered activities, in age-group clusters, both in school, little league, and all of those things, than they do interacting across different levels of maturity.

3. *Lack of Respect for Developmental Stages*

In the previous chapter we discussed the importance of developmental readiness. Developmental readiness is an important factor to consider in helping children develop all of the *significant seven* perceptions, capabilities, and skills and will be discussed here as it relates to developing judgement skills.

People go through fairly predictable stages in acquiring conventional human reasoning and judgement. Parents need to recognize and allow for basic stages of cognitive development which influence the development of judgmental skills.

Terry was an extremely bright two-year-old. One Saturday evening he attended a drive-in movie with his parents. Two weeks later he was riding in the car with his father when they passed the same drive-in theater. Terry recognized it and commented, "We went there last night." His father stopped the car and gave Terry a spanking for lying.

This father did not understand cognitive development. Terry showed highly developed perceptive skills to recognize the location of the movie two weeks after he had been there. He had not yet developed a clear understanding of time. He did not have the cognitive maturity to understand the difference between last night and two weeks ago. He was not lying.

The ability to use judgement and control one's own behavior requires some ability to anticipate consequences in the future. The ability to focus attention increases with age, as does the ability to understand causal relationships and to anticipate future events. The following example further illustrates this point:

Suppose we give a two-year-old the choice of a candy bar in one hand and a $100 bill in the other hand. She will take the candy every time. Give an eight year old the same choice, and the $100 bill will win every time. If we ask the two-year-old why she chose the candy, she won't even understand the question. If we ask the eight-year-old, she will quickly tell us that she can buy many, many candy bars with $100.

We need to be aware of when children are ready to use judgement. Some parents think they must spank a two-year-old to teach her not to run in the street. Yet, these same parents would not be willing to let that child play unsupervised near a busy street. Most parents have enough judgement to know that the child has not developed enough judgement to handle that situation no matter how many spankings she has had. So, obviously, the spanking is for the parents' benefit, not the child's.

A responsible parent will simply restrain a small child from running into the street by close supervision and hand-holding when necessary and then take every opportunity to engage the child in dialogue and collaboration when the child is ready: "What do we need to watch for before we cross the street? How many ways do we need to look before we know it is safe? What might happen if we don't look both ways and a car hit us?"

An understanding of developmental stages based on the work of Piaget and Kolberg and explained in the chart on the following page helps parents know what expectations are reasonable and the level of skill development for which the child is ready.

Today the teen years offer new developmental considerations. Thirty five years ago adolescence was not considered a troublesome period. The word *teenager* did not even appear in American dictionaries until the mid 1950's. When children were needed literally for economic survival, they had so much responsibility placed on them at a very early age that by the time they reached twelve, they often had similar skills and responsibilities as most adults. They did not have much time to be influenced by peers with too much time on their hands. They did not have the influence of television, drugs, and the freedom offered by automobiles. Dealing with the new feelings and emotions of puberty was much less complicated in a more stable environment.

AGE	TYPE OF THINKING	JUDGMENT TYPES PRINCIPLES
0-2	Sensorimotor	World of here and now. Pain - Pleasure Can - Can't
2-6	Pre-operational	Sees only one aspect at a time. Thinking is rigid. Black - White Safe - Dangerous
6-11	Concrete	Begins to understand relationships. Able to use logical thought only when solving problems involving concrete objects and events.
11+	Abstract	Cause & Effect Legal - Illegal What will happen if ____? Capable of dealing with the hypothetical. Discriminates abstract concepts. Appropriate - Inappropriate Fair - Unfair How will ____ feel about ____?

However, due to the transitions discussed in Chapter One, most teenagers experience the stages listed below as they move through adolescence, according to Dr. Robert L. Hendren.

When parents do not understand the normal stages of adolescence, they are likely to feel inadequate as parents or to use adultisms: "How come you never? Why can't you ever? Surely you realize! Why don't you grow up?" This kind of non-support from parents only increases feelings in teenagers of inadequacy and the need for peer support to find meaning, purpose, and relevance.

EARLY ADOLESCENCE (12 to 14 years)

1. Begin questioning parent's value.
2. Are often moody.
3. Form closer friendships. Would rather go out with their friends then be with their parents.
4. Realize parents aren't perfect — identify their faults.
5. Follow interests and clothing styles of peer groups.

MIDDLE ADOLESCENCE (14 to 17 years)

1. Become self-involved, alternating between unrealistically high expectations and poor self-concept.
2. Complain that parents interfere with independence.
3. Are extremely concerned with appearance and with their bodies. Start primping and strutting their stuff.
4. Have a lower opinion of parents — withdraw emotionally from them, form sense of identity from peer group.

LATE ADOLESCENCE (17 TO 19 years)

1. Firmer identity. Have a better sense of who they are and what they stand for.
2. Become better at expressing feelings with words.
3. Have a more developed sense of humor.
4. Are more emotionally stable. Don't have the wide mood swings of previous stages.
5. Take more pride in their work — more self-reliant.

GAINS CAN BE LOST DURING ADOLESCENCE

Many elementary schools today offer excellent substance abuse education programs. It is not unusual to hear a 10 or 11-year-old say with great clarity, "I will never be dumb enough to smoke or drink or use drugs. I don't want to do that to my body."

Parents often give a sigh of relief and think they have it made. They think they can now relax and trust their children's judgement forever more.

When these same kids reach 13 and 14-years-of age and start staying out late with all kinds of seemingly valid excuses, or come home stoned, parents are confused and often feel like a failure or try to deny that a problem exists because, "My child said he would never do such a thing." An understanding of the developmental stages can decrease the confusion and offer guidelines for action.

When teenagers are going through these stages, they are even more in need of experience and practice in developing the *significant seven*. They need to know that we understand their feelings, but that we also understand the dangers of this time in their life and that we will continue to offer firmness with dignity and respect because of our great love and concern for them. They need to be involved in family traditions and family meetings where they feel a climate of support rather than the win/lose position. Adults need to increase their efforts in encouraging the development of judgmental skills to help children survive this turbulent period of their life.

BUILDERS FOR DEVELOPING JUDGEMENT

1. *Provide Dialogue and Collaboration*

The primary vehicle through which judgement is acquired is collaboration and dialogue between the less mature and the more mature through the use of the EIAG process as children mature through the developmental stages. For years we assumed these stages would occur automatically.

The old farmer, in the world we came from, realized the importance of teaching his son about the primary business of the family. He knew that how well his son learned what he had learned would ultimately determine the success and survival of the family if anything happened to him. He realized that there would be time when he would have to stop directing, "It is time to cut the hay," and say to his son, "If you had to decide whether we cut the hay or not today, what would you look for? What do you think?"

He would listen to his son's judgement, "I think we should cut it, Dad," and then check further, "Well, what about that thunderhead coming over the mountain?"

"Gee, I didn't look at the sky. I was looking at the grass, Dad."

"Well, what will happen if you get all this hay cut and then that thunderhead brings a big rain?"

"It will ruin all the hay."

In that way the father challenged the son to develop his judgmental skills. That is what the old apprenticeship model did. Ultimately the apprentice had to choose some wood sometimes, and even go about the task of making something, and then find that he had misjudged the grain after he got it all built and it broke. Just like the daughter sometimes had to be allowed to stitch a whole button-hole into the fabric of a shirt the wrong way in the grain of the material, and then watch it split the first time she buttoned it, to very graphically become aware of the consequences of poor choices.

We have preempted allowing young people to learn from experience. It is easier to lecture, instruct, explain, and moralize, which does not promote moral and ethical development, critical thinking, judgmental maturity, and comprehension.

2. *Provide Role-taking Opportunities*

Role-taking occurs when we place children in the role of the decision maker and let them attempt to apply their knowledge, experience, and insight to an actual or a valid hypothetical situation in order to test their insight and understanding.

Role-taking was first described by Lawrence Kohlberg in his studies of cognitive and moral development. It is an apprenticeship in thinking and discovering wisdom.

Judgmental skills develop when parents, teachers, and others create or allow children to get into situations from which they cannot escape except through thinking. This is effective only when adults can then have the patience and courage to allow to use their thinking skills to solve their own problems.

Parents can help their children develop judgmental skills by providing role-taking experiences for them as early as possible. Allow them to take the role of decision-maker with small things that are safe for them to handle, that have only the power to inconvenience them, not seriously impair them. It is important to accept the choices made without taking them away because we don't like the decision that was made.

DON'T GIVE AND THEN TAKE AWAY

I observed the process done very poorly recently. I was at a shoe store, and I heard a parent say, "You can choose your new shoes."

The child ran and got an expensive pair of cowboy boots. The parent said, "I didn't mean those." This statement immediately impugned the child's judgement. Then, in a peak, she walked over and grabbed two pair of tennis shoes on sale, plunked them down, and said, "Choose one of these."

My ten-year-old son, standing beside me said, "Dad, he won't wear either pair."

Family closets are filled with things that should be taken to Goodwill because parents purchased them for *practical* reasons when their children had chosen something else. Children get even by ignoring the things their parents have chosen.

The parent could have said, "I have set aside $15.00 to get you some shoes. You may go through the store and choose the pair you want for that amount or less. Whatever you choose you will have to get by with for three months until I can afford to replace them."

As I left the shoe store, I heard another mother say to a child, "You can choose where we have lunch."

The child choose a fast food place. The mother immediately came back with, "But honey, they have such a nice salad bar at this other restaurant."

The child said, "But I want to go here."

The mother followed up with, "You know I like salad at this time of the day," already manipulating, pulling the rug out from under the child, and impugning his judgement. That was a very poor way to proceed. This incident will teach the child to avoid making choices and to have less confidence in the ones he does make.

In earlier chapters we pointed out that when adults choose to explore a child's perception of an event, they validate and affirm and encourage the child. But in the very act of exploring the what?, the why and the how?, we are also teaching the child to analyze situations.

3. *Provide Opportunities For Children to Experience the Consequences of Choices*

We help young people develop judgement when we are willing to allow them to choose poorly, experience the consequences of having the shoes fall apart, and let them get by until the time is up.

We had this experience with Kimbi, our yuppie, preppie daughter. We gave her a back-to-school-clothes allotment. Then with the confidence and clarity found only in fourteen year olds, she rushed out and decided that in place of several interchangeable pieces of clothing, that one Ralph Lauren original would be the thing to start high school in. We carefully explored the implications of that. "Honey, have you considered day in and day out what kinds of things you will have to wear?"

"Yes I have, Dad. This is real neat and real important. This is what a kid should have."

We also asked, "Do you understand when your next allotment will come to obtain school clothes?" She verified that she understood that it was the following December and it was now the beginning of September. Once we had gone through that, she went out and obtained her Ralph Lauren original.

Within a week she was so bored with that outfit, and her friends were even asking her if she at least washed it. It touched off a great round of creativity. Having no budget, she successfully managed to glean some extra large shirts that I had marginally worn out, got out the sewing machine, put drawstrings in them, cut flaps, and put buttons on so she had coverlets and shields. She made it somehow until December. When she received her next school clothes allotment, she went out and bought several interchangeable outfits of dubious status in order to have a little more flexibility.

We would have set aside all of that important learning and validation if we had felt sorry for her and gone out and got her a new wardrobe while pointing out the deficiencies in her judgement. But by allowing her to experience things that could only produce inconvenience and a little embarrassment, she became more confident, more self-assured. When she went out to shop again, she showed better judgement and a clearer understanding of what she was doing. She is less likely in the future to go off half-cocked with that first blush assurance and will ask, "What else is there here that I have not considered?"

LEARNING FROM MISTAKES

Some parents are afraid their children will totally lose their confidence and have low self-esteem by choosing poorly. Actually, quite the contrary occurs. When young people truly believe that their choices affect outcomes, they feel potent and significant and become increasingly confident that they have some of the reins of their life. They become more adept in holding these reins and become better human beings.

4. *Encourage Reflection Upon the What?, Why?, and How?*

The first step in making judgments is to know how to analyze situations and to know what questions to ask to find insight. The what, the why, and the how of a situation give people the basic material to begin to make a judgement.

Children must learn to understand what is significant in a situation, why it is significant, and how it could affect what happens. They can then use their knowledge, insight, and experience to guide them in determining what to do about it.

It takes training in analysis, and then training and practice in application of ideas and wisdom, to ultimately arrive at judgement.

The evening of the day we had been at the shoe store I had an experience with my son. He came up to me and said, "Dad, Mom says you are going to be away for a couple of weeks. I was thinking, wouldn't it be so nice to go to the amusement park on this weekend?"

I said, "Son, that sounds real good." Then I took this opportunity to allow him to do some role-taking and said, "Why don't I show you what I have to do to decide whether we can do it or not. The first thing I have to decide is how much money we would have to have to take on the trip. Why don't you think of each of the things we will need to do? Then I will put a price to it, and we will see how much the trip would cost."

We estimated the gas, the admission and the food, and came up with a budget that was about $40. Then I told him, "The second thing I have to do is look at what money we have on hand and what our priorities are at the present time." At that time we were building an addition on our home and had been cursed with good weather, so the contractors were running way ahead of schedule and squeezing us for every dime to pay our way. So I went through all the things we had to do that month and came up with what we had left, which was about $30.

Then, instead of making the decision for him, I said, "Son, since you know what the budget is, and you know what we have on hand that we can use, why don't you put yourself in my situation. If you had to tell me whether we could go or not, what would your decision be, and what would be your reasons for making it?"

He looked it over and said, "Dad, I don't think we can go because we need $10 more to be able to go."

I said, "Son, that is my conclusion too. And while I really wish it were different, that it our situation, and I am sure you understand it."

He said, "I do, Dad," and he ran off to play.

That night I was getting ready for bed. As I was pulling off my boots, he came into see me and said, "Dad, I've been thinking about that trip to the amusement park."

I said, "So have I son, and I wish there was a way to do it."

He said, "After you showed me your priorities, I want away and said to myself, 'Mike, what are your priorities?' I decided I have lots of baseball and football cards and not too many opportunities to put together a trip with you. So, I traded off some of my baseball cards for some discount coupons to the amusement park and I have saved us $12. Not only can we go, but we can have two hot dogs that we didn't allow for in our budget."

Did he get to go? Yes he did. And I believe that he is showing quite a bit of growth in the *significant seven* as we have discussed in the past seven chapters.

PUTTING ALL THE SIGNIFICANT SEVEN TOGETHER

1. Michael does believe at age ten that he is a capable person who can find a way to do things if he will try.

2. He believes he can contribute significantly to a relationship that is important to him through his creativity, his ideas, and his resourcefulness.

3. Does he believe that when circumstances occur which could prevent him from getting his way that he is powerless and needs to have a temper tantrum? Or does he believe that he can find a way to creatively alter those circumstances, or alter his response to them, so that he has power and influence over his environment?

4. He shows some ability for self-assessment, self-control and self-discipline in sorting out "feel like it" and "want it."

5. He shows ability to communicate, cooperate, negotiate, share, empathize and listen.

6. He shows some understanding of limits and consequences, privileges and responsibilities, cause and effect, and his role in dealing with them.

7. He shows some ability to apply abstract notions such as afford, can't afford, reasonable, and unreasonable in responding to a given life situation.

At age ten, Michael already believes he is capable, significant, and influential. He is developing the skills and capabilities to help him be successful in anything that he sets his mind to accomplish. He is already showing problem-solving skills, initiative, creativity, and the ability to negotiate, make a deal.

Did all that happen automatically?" No. The development of these skills and capabilities was a product of lots of time spent with EIAG, exploring when we could have explained, encouraging and inviting when we could have directed, checking things out instead of assuming, celebrating what he did accomplish instead of hitting him over the head with what he didn't, and instead of requiring mind reading with "Surely you realize we can't go if we can't afford it," showing respect, "Son, what is your understanding of what that would mean to our situation?"

Mike is a capable young person developing maturity and judgement and had benefited from his parents' struggles with older sisters and foster children as they learned to parent without networks and other support systems.

LOVING SUPPORT WITHOUT RESCUING

The next morning his 19-year-old sister came and sat on the bed, obviously wanting to talk. "What's up?" I said.

"Oh Dad, I don't know what to do. I have a good job offer, but I've also been accepted at college, and I don't know what to do!"

We discussed her perceptions of the relative strengths and weakness of each option. When we finished she said, "What should I do Daddy?"

I said, "Honey, it's a decision only you can make."

She said, "Dad, I've been making decisions my whole life. Couldn't you make just this one?"

With a full heart I said, "Dear, I have learned that decisions are your life, and I have seen you make some good ones and some not so good ones, but you have always learned from them and have gone on with life. This is one that you must live with when you make it, and I love you too much to take the choice from you."

"Oh Daddy," she said. "I know you love me and that I must chose. I guess I just needed to share some of the struggle with you."

For now, she has chosen and will choose again and again, for that is how capable people live.

Chapter 11

BLUEPRINT FOR SUCCESS

One of the leading predictors of success for young people — their performance in life, their motivation, their health, and their productivity — is their perception of their parent's perceptions and expectations of them — not necessarily what parents believe about them, but what they believe their parents believe about them.

It is important to understand that what parents believe about their children and what children believe their parents believe about them are often very different beliefs. For example, a child may bring a paper home from school with the perception that, "This is the best job I've ever done on a paper. I'll bet my parents will be very proud of me."

The perceptions of the parents of this child would be compatible if they said, "Honey, this is the best job you've ever done on a paper. We're really satisfied with the effort you have put it."

Instead, the parents have the belief that, "I should always point out things to help my child do better because that is what love is — to make sure people do their best."

The child takes the paper and goes away depressed, feeling, "Even when I've done my best, it is never good enough for my parents." The child perceives the event as a demonstration of rejections while the parents interpret it as an act of love.

This kind of misunderstanding can be crucial since the strength or weakness of children's perceptions of closeness and trust in their relationships with parents and teachers can determine the course of their life. When young people do not feel closeness and trust with significant adults, they usually turn to their peers.

CLOSENESS AND TRUST

Research from the Search Institute has shown that peer influence is closely linked to the rise in rebellion, resistance to culture, chemical abuse, and promiscuity. Children who have strong perceptions of closeness and trust with significant adults are very resistant to peer influence and are more influenced by those adults who validate them for who they are.

The Search Institute conducted an extensive study in which they asked young people, "If you had a serious problem in your life, who would you prefer to discuss it with in order to get help and gain insight?" The overwhelming results indicated that young people would prefer to talk to their parents.

However, when asked who they felt they actually could go to in order to be listened to and taken seriously, the consensus was, "No matter how much I wish I could go to my parents, I could not. They already act towards me as if I am dumb, stupid, and inadequate and seem to feel that I am always letting them down. My friends are the only ones who will listen to me and take me seriously, so I talk with them even though I know they don't know any more about life that I do."

Young people feel closeness and trust when significant adults listen to them, take them seriously, and give them affirmation for what they are doing. If parents replaced just one, "Why can't you ever?" with, "Honey, let me be sure I understand what it was you thought I wanted," closeness and trust would be enhanced.

Most of the concepts presented in this book are designed to promote closeness and trust, such as eliminating the barriers and applying the builders, practicing firmness with dignity and respect, involving children in the decision making process, giving them meaningful roles and on-the-job training, and structuring consequences — all or which lead to closeness and trust.

Perceptions of closeness and trust can be measured by a wonderful new instrument which has been developed by Fred Streit after many years of studying relationships between family members.

EPAC (EXPECTATIONS, PERCEPTIONS, ASSESSMENT, AND CHANGE)

EPAC is an accurate inventory which will draw an 85% reliable picture of a relationship by measuring the 26 most critical elements of personal relationships and assigning a relative weight to those elements. People can take this inventory to assess how they are doing in creating closeness and trust according to the perceptions of those they supposedly love.

EPAC measures perceptions. Perceptions of the perceptions of others is also important in adult relationships. The best predictor of stress, productivity, and wellness in a couple's relationship is determined by what each member of that couple believes the other member of that couple believes about and expects of him or her.

EPAC is also a prescriptive tool that will give guidance on what to do in all the areas in which stress or misunderstanding is building up, either between husband and wife or between children and parents.

THE DEVELOPMENT OF EPAC

During the process of refining the instrument, the researchers initially took several thousand 11 to 18 year old young people in a public school setting and administered the instrument to them. Based only on their pattern of responses to the instrument, these young people were differentiated clearly into three categories:

1. High risk to involvement in the problem areas for teenagers.

2. Clearly low risk to involvement in the problem areas.

3. No significant tendency either way.

Then the researchers went to the records and found that 90% of the young people declared high risk by the instrument had very high rates of involvement in drug and alchohol abuse, school absenteeism, disciplinary referrals, under achievement, and agency contacts. They found that 85% of the young people declared low risk by the instrument were in the opposite situation. They had high levels of achievement and productivity and minimal involvement in any of the problem areas.

The scientists doing the research decided that they could not assume that there would be a general trend of improvement in relationships between children and their parents without some intervention. So with the hypotheses that there would generally be no significant upward movement without intervention, they predicted what the children would be like at age 16 based on their pattern of responses at age eleven.

After testing these eleven-year-old children, they split them into two groups. One group was not given intervention methods. The parents and teachers of the children in the other group were informed what the instrument showed and received specific guidance as to how they could intervene.

When these children reached the age of 16, they were retested. Ninety percent of the adolescents in the control group which did not receive intervention were in the extreme high risk category, as predicted. They were involved in the problem areas for teenagers. Only 15% of the other children who received intervention based on the insight gained from EPAC were in the high risk category when they reached 16 years of age.

Even though intervention began during the most turbulent and difficult time of puberty, these young people completely reversed the pattern they had begun toward being high risk in problem areas.

On the way to polishing the instrument, the scientists found another interesting thing. They tested 4,000 chemically dependent individuals in treatment between the ages of 11 and 45.

Most chemically dependent people have a primary drug of choice. If they can't get what they want, they will use whatever they can get. But left on their own, they will generally specialize. The researchers knew the primary drug of choice for each of the chemically dependent people tested.

The researchers were able to sort out 85% of the individuals in the sample who did not use any drugs or alcohol. These non-users were immediately evident based on their responses to EPAC. The researchers went a step further and claimed they could predict the primary drug choice for these chemically dependent individuals by knowing how they perceived their relationship with their parents. The researchers were accurate on 65% of the primary marijuana dependent individuals in the sample, which is fairly high given the peer pressure to use marijuana.

They jumped to 95% accuracy with hallucinogen and in-halant abusers and 100% reliability in spotting heroin addicts. The EPAC instrument can spot a potential heroin addict in eleven year old children very consistently.

They were 95% reliable identifying the alcohol, sedative, and cocaine individuals just based on their pattern of responses to the instrument regarding four variables: strictness, permissiveness, love, and hostility.

STRICTNESS VS. PERMISSIVENESS

EPAC plots two variables having to do with control issues in parenting — strictness and permissiveness. The results are shown in the pie diagram in Figure A.

Permissiveness, at the top of the pie, is defined as excessive autonomy. There is too little structure and too little predictability in the relationship. These parents easily give in when children hassle and manipulate.

The opposite of permissiveness, shown at the bottom of the pie, is excessive control or strictness which has been defined in an earlier chapter as too much imposition of power and authority over another person. Excessive control or strictness will usually produce rebellion, resistance, hostility, and aggression, which leave children at high risk to become involved in one or more of the problems areas.

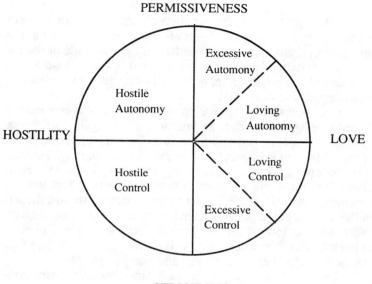

Figure A

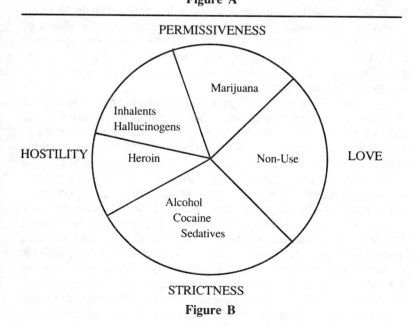

Figure B

LOVE VS. HOSTILITY

EPAC plots two other variables having to do with issues of love and hostility on the part of parents which are illustrated in the pie diagram in Figure A. Love is plotted on the right side of the pie diagram and is defined as caring, interest, and respect. Hostility, on the left side of the pie diagram, is defined as neglect, lack of caring, lack of interest, and disrespect.

Four poles, then, appear on the diagram. The researchers polarized love against hostility and permissiveness against strictness. Halfway between love and strictness is loving control. Toward the right top of the pie is bias in favor of excessive autonomy. Halfway between loving and permissive is loving autonomy. Toward the right bottom of the pie is bias in favor of excessive control. Halfway between loving and strictness is loving control. Moving toward the left from the bottom of the pie bias again is in favor of strictness but with hostility. Moving toward the left from the top of the pie is bias toward permissiveness with hostility. It is on the left side that we find the range between hostile autonomy and hostile control.

The middle right of the pie (a balance between loving control and loving autonomy) indicates the low risk area of relationships. When young people perceive the control parents exercise over them as being within the range of loving control designed to move toward loving autonomy and believe overall that there is evidence of love, care, and respect as the dominate theme, then they experience a low risk, stable, relatively low stress relationship. Turbulence begins when the balance between loving control and loving autonomy is passed in either direction.

The pie diagram in Figure B illustrates the common drug of choice as a result of perceptions usually developed by young people in response to each type of parenting. Negative behaviors such as manipulation, disrespect, a poor attitude toward life and learning, promiscuity, excessive peer influence, marijuana, and hallucinogen abuse cluster in the loving autonomy piece of the pie. When parents err predominately in favor of permissiveness, they can expect those behaviors in relative degrees, depending on how permissive they are.

Behaviors such as rebellion, resistance, hostility, aggression, frequent vandalism, sexual acting out, alcohol, cocaine, and sedatives abuse fall in the strictness quadrant of the pie. Hostile control (any control that is not loving and respectful) is a very expensive strategy for both children and adults. Parents who err predominately in favor of strictness with hostility can expect those behaviors in relative degress depending on the degree of hostility and strictness as perceived by children.

Parents may be strict because they feel that being strict is the most loving thing they can do for their children. However, their children may not perceive the loving part. *Children base their behavior on their perceptions of what is true, not on what is actually true.* Children are more likely to perceive loving intentions when tone of voice and actions convey dignity and respect along with firmness.

Extremely abherent sexual behavior and self-degrading acting out behaviors and heroin abuse fall on the left side of the pie in the area of hostile autonomy.

MOVING GRADUALLY FROM LOVING CONTROL TO LOVING AUTONOMY

Children usuaully reach a high level of maturity, self- discipline, and responsibility and become strong in the *significant seven* when we guide them from loving control to loving autonomy on a schedule they are developmentally ready for.

Younger children need more loving control. As children mature and are ready and able to handle more responsibility, they are ready for more loving autonomy. The children who experience this process of parenting, which gradually shifts from loving control to loving autonomy, are most likely to perceive closeness and trust in their relationships with their parents. The results of this kind of parenting for children are high levels of productivity, achievment, and resistance to negative peer influence.

The following vignettes give an example of parenting styles within each of the four quadrants of the pie chart. Each parent is responding to a request to spend the weekend with a friend.

A parent who uses *hostile autonomy* might say, "Hey, whatever. We will see you around." This teenager gets to do what she wants to do, but the parent shows lack of interest and lack of involvement and is very laissez faire. Caring is absent.

A parent who uses *loving autonomy* might say, "Son, I know you have to put together your schedule for the weekend, but I would appreciate it if you would let me know what you decide." This teenager also gets to do what he wants but does not have any guidelines and does not need to show any responsibility.

A parent who uses *hostile control* might say, "You know better than that. You're grounded for a month. Maybe two months. You may never go out again as long as you live." This teenager is on restriction but is filled with hostility because love and respect are lacking.

A parent who uses *loving control* might say, "Sounds like fun to me. Let me know your plans and what you think is a reasonable time for you to come home. Then I will give my ideas on what is reasonable. When we are in agreement, we will go over the consequences of what will happen if you are late. Then I will call the parents of your friend to make sure an adult will be available at all times."

Many parents have objected that the latter dialogue will not work with teenagers. Many of these parents are used to giving in to hassling and manipulating of young people or use hostile control. Teenagers may not respond to a firm but loving approach at first when they are used to other extremes. Confidence on the part of parents is a primary key.

The latter dialogue is very effective with teen-agers when it is done with confidence, love, concern, a tone of voice that shows dignity and respect, and unwavering patience.

We have presented a model in this book which allows us to control the variables of control versus permissiveness and love versus hostility which are so important in influencing young people. The methods we have presented allow a parent or teacher to exercise control more firmly but with increasing dignity and respect so young people will perceive control as supportive rather than a barrier or an act of aggression. These methods lead to the development of skills and perceptions of capability that allow parents and teachers to move toward more loving autonomy.

IT IS NEVER TOO LATE

We have heard many parents say, "Good grief! I have already made so many mistakes. Is it too late?"

It is never too late. We have stressed throughout this book that any improvement will show improved results. The EPAC instrument demonstrated that intervention was successful in 85% of the cases.

It is very easy to err in the direction of permissiveness or strictness. I once had the tendency is to err in the permissiveness direction because I am so opposed to the humiliation children often experience through strictness. I would often simply add dignity and respect to firmness but too many times would go to the other extreme with what I then perceived as loving autonomy. It was really excessive permissiveness.

During the writing of this book I had the opportunity to learn the truth of these principles by paying a very difficult price.

I learned that my son was engaging in most of the behaviors

associated with excessive permissiveness, including the use of marijuana. In my zeal to correct the situation, I over-corrected and became excessively strict which my son interpreted as hostility and intensified some of his acting out behaviors.

My son and his friend gave up marijuana, but because I did not work on correcting the weakness in perceptions and capabilities that led to the drug abuse in the first place and simply became excessively strict, they accelerated their rebellious behavior and decided to try a halucinogen drug. They had heard from friends that if they took eight motion sickness pills they would experience a *real trip*.

They had pitched a tent on an island in a lake about 200 yards from shore and the family camper. The first night was uneventful. We checked on them several times during the day to see if they needed anything or if they wanted to come to shore. They declined, indicating that they were having a good time learning survival skills.

The second night they each took eight of the pills and soon started hallucinating. Because of the effects of the drug, it was difficult to obtain a clear story of what happened during the night, but apparently they did not enjoy the experience as much as they thought they would and decided to try to sleep it off.

In the wee hours of the morning they woke up, each having separate hallucinations. My son's friend tried to swim for shore but did not make it. He drowned.

This was a difficult way for all of us to learn — an extremely high price to pay. Jimmy's parents felt very strongly impressed during a family prayer that Jimmy's mission in life had been fulfilled — that his death might serve as a message to save others. I wrote the following poem for Jimmy:

Jimmy is dead.
His friends and loved ones grieve.
He was such a joy!
We were not ready for him to leave.

But Jimmy gave his life
That perhaps one more might live.
His mission even greater
If tens or hundreds learn and live.

It was only a motion sickness pill.
But "friends" said, "Take eight
If you want a real thrill —
A 'trip' that is really great."

These "friends" were too blind to see
The dangers of this "high."
"Don't think of consequences.
Have fun now, and fly."

"What do parents know?
They just want to spoil our fun.
They talk about the future.
Who cares! Now is our time in the sun!"

And so, Jimmy is dead.
But he speaks from the grave:
"My death will not be in vain
If even one of you it saves."

"Please tell all your friends
So even more might hear.
Kids are not as smart as they think
When they ignore what their parents fear."

"Tell everyone you see.
Let all your friends know.
Parents hassle you about drugs
Because they love you so."

"My mission on earth is over.
But please join now with me.
Let my death give meaning to your message.
Together we can help others be free."

"Free to think for themselves.
Free to listen to those who know.
Free to have courage —
And know when it is smart to say, 'No!'"

"Do not grieve for me.
I am in a wonderful place above.
But do not forget my message:
'Get high on life and love!'"

It is easy to say that mistakes are opportunities to learn, but it is sometimes difficult to believe when we are in the middle of experiencing the consequences. It takes true understanding and insight to be able to focus on solutions rather than blame.

I called Steve, 3000 miles away, to tell him what had happened. I said, "If you want me to withdraw from this book writing project, I would understand why you might not want my name associated with what you are doing."

Steve very perceptively replied, "Now more than ever. What you learn from this and share with others can be very helpful to so many."

It was at this time that Steve suggested to simply eliminate *the barriers* and to engage in *closet listening*. These two very simple activities (simple because they both essentially mean to *not do anything* intentionally but to be open and sensitive to what is already there) have resulted in a total change in my relationship with my son.

Eliminating the barriers and quietly listening created an environment of support. He opened up and talked more than I thought was possible. When he felt listened to and taken seriously, he was then willing to listen — especially since what I had to say did not include any of the barriers.

The closeness and trust we have developed as a result of this experience has resulted in some dramatic changes for both of us. We have both made some lifestyle changes for the better.

I have told him, with confidence and concern, that I will actively engage in building *networks* with the parents of his friends and that I will check with other parents to make sure adult supervision is available whenever he is away from home because I understand the dangers of peer pressure even when he *knows better.*

Our family meetings have included discussions of the importance and significance of our children's contributions. During these meetings we carefully structure responsibilities for every privilege.

I have learned the importance of *taking the time* to simply *hang out* in the same room with my children, to be available to answer their questions, to watch television together so we can follow-up with discussions, to play a game together, to simply enjoy them as individuals.

These principles do work to develop capable young people no matter when or where we start.

THE ALCHOLOLIC'S ANONYMOUS PROCESS

Perhaps the most relevant insight into the process of developing capable people comes from a careful analysis of the changes occurring in individuals who succeed in the treatment and recovery process through Alcoholics Anonymous. When we compare the two and a half million people in 50 years who have gone from dependent, vulnerable, inadequate people to capable, growing, stable people, with people who went through the exact same program but did not make changes, we see the following results for the successful people:

The first step to recovery is a perceptual change from, "I am the way I am," to "I am capable of learning to be different. I am capable of taking the initiative in my life."

The second step to recovery is a perceptual change from, "My life is meaningless, and I don't matter to anyone anyway," to, "There is a power greater than myself that gives life meaning and purpose, and I have significance when I contribute to the recovery process of others."

The third step is acquiring the perception that "Although I am powerless over chemicals, I am not powerless over the choices that bring them into my life. Until I accept responsibility for my choices, I will always be a victim. I can be a victor when I accept responsibility that I cannot control all circumstances of my life, but I can control what I do about circumstances or what I allow myself to feel about them."

Once people believe they are capable, significant, and potentially influential in their lives (the first three perceptions of the *significant seven*), the process of Alcoholic Anonymous then helps them practice all four of the *significant seven* skills.

When we identify the changes in perceptions and the changes in skills that occur in these successful people, we have a basic understanding of the core of the habilitation process which can serve as a base for effective prevention and intervention programs as well as the treatment process.

This possible convergence of prevention, intervention, and treatment was understood by Dr. Bob and Bill W. (withholding their last names to preserve their anonymity) over fifty years ago when they wrote in the first edition of *The Blue Book of Alcoholic's Anonymous* that, "These are essential principles that we must share with our entire culture, and especially the alcoholic." They became concerned that their zeal to save the culture would overshadow the needs of the alcoholic, so later editions of the Blue Book omitted any reference to sharing with the entire culture.

Principles that have been proven successful in helping people in many different programs are usually universal principles that will help people everywhere.

DON'T OVERLOOK DRUGS

A tragic fact of live for Americans is the fact that we are the worlds leading consumer of illicit and elicit drugs. Their general availability and widespread use make them a major barrier to children and adults realizing their potential.

All the activities and principles in this book have been shown to be significant contributors to prevention, intervention and treatment processes. However, there is no substitute for an informed, aware parent who actively develops a child's understanding of how and when to confront peer pressures and situations associated with chemical use.

Alcoholism and other patterns of chemical dependency show a strong hereditary pattern which requires us to know and share with our children our family history. There are many families and individuals for whom the only responsible use is *no use* and there is no responsible use of alcohol and psycho-active drugs, such as hallucinogens, marijuana and cocaine, except under medical supervision during the developmental years from 0 to 20 Human development is a very sensitive chemical and bio- physiological process during the growth years and puberty.

Our knowledge of these issues is expanding constantly and patterns of drug use change consistently with fads and new chemicals. For this reason, most books and pamphlets are dated before they are published.

Parents and other concerned individuals are well advised to form a relationship with local, state, and national groups seeking to keep the public informed. The following general list should provide sufficient information to obtain newsletters and contact information for local groups in any area of the country:

The White House Office for Drug Abuse Policy The National Institute on Drug Abuse (NIDA) The National Institute on Alcoholism (NIAAA) The National Federation of Parents for Drug Free Youth (NFP) Parent Resources in Drug Education (PRIDE)

PRIDE offers a toll-free telephone number for their Action Pride Drug Information System. 800-241-9746 can be called 24 hours a day.

In addition to the above organizations every state has designated drug abuse and alcoholism abuse prevention coordinators who can be reached either through NIDA above or by contacting your state government.

People often ask, "How soon should we start to become aware and active in dealing with the phenomenon of drug abuse?" We believe that it should be a consideration from early childhood on since television and other media begin exposing children to drug taking and drinking with the onset of consciousness. Hundreds of thousands of parents waited until adolescence only to discover the exposure began much earlier and the best times for prevention had past before they were aware of the need. Basically *if you care, be aware!*

It is our hope that people who read this book will begin to recognize that successful emergence through adolescence and success in confronting the issues of chemicals in our culture hinges on learning to encourage the *significant seven* in all of our relationships.

EPAC is available through:
People Science
168 Woodbridge Ave.
Highland Park, NJ   08904

Chapter 12

THE PRICE OF CHANGE

What price are we as adults willing to pay for the quality of young people's preparation for their future and ours? Will Rogers, who was sought out at another time of great social upheaval for his wisdom, taught it this way:

"Quality is a lot like buying oats. If you want fresh, clean, first quality oats, you have to pay a fair price. But if you can be satisfied with oats that have been through the horse, they come a lot cheaper."

We have outlined the cost of quality as we understand it. If we decide not to pay the price, we can't be so critical of those that we serve for having more manure in their life than quality.

The changes represented by transition are here to stay. These changes have created the problems we have outlined, but they have also created unlimited opportunities. Since we know how to compensate for the problems that have been created, *now* is definitely the best of times for our children to reach their full success potential.

However, compensating for the problems that have been created means that adults must become personally converted to a different set of priorities and activities in their classrooms and homes to help children develop the skills and capabilities that were once developed more naturally in past environments. Everything has its price.

WILLINGNESS TO PAY THE PRICE

We see a great willingness to pay this price. This willingness is increasing. Each year we travel throughout the United States and to many countries. We have witnessed a great shift in the openness and desire of adults to become informed and involved in the process of helping young people. More parents and educators than ever before are now willing to make the changes necessary to increase the productivity and joy of their efforts once they know what changes produce effective results.

INSURANCE

We understand the concept of insurance. We can take out insurance against hazards close at home if we:

1. Maintain closeness and trust.

2. Use firmness with dignity and respect.

3. Don't misuse affluence.

4. Teach children the capabilities they need to achieve success and happiness.

New skills often feel awkward at first. Many of us remember when we first learned to ride a bicycle! As children we usually did not let awkwardness stop us. We were too excited about the possibilities of what we would be able to do with our new skills.

Think of the new possibilities for closeness and trust we will feel in our relationships with our children and others when we learn the skills outlined in this book. It won't be quite so scary and awkward if we go slowly and take one step at a time.

ONE STEP AT A TIME

The first step is to change our own perceptions of how to obtain closeness and trust. We must change our attitudes which promote *demands* and *threats* to attitudes which promote *warmth, interest,* and *invitation.*

EASY DOES IT

The second step is to practice slowly. We might even start by being a *closet listeners.* We can practice listening without even letting anyone know what we are doing.

Part of being a *closet listener* is to eliminate the five barriers which were discussed in Chapter 4. It is impossible to listen while we are still using the barriers. We can become aware of how much we accomplish by doing *nothing* on purpose. Then *nothing* can be a very important *something.*

GETTING INTO THE CHILD'S WORLD

The third step is to practice understanding the perceptions of young people. This will come much easier when we are truly interested and when we truly listen to their point of view.

Once we have mastered *closet listening*, we can practice understanding perceptions through the EIAG process: "Let me be sure I understand. How do you see the situation? What things do you see happening for you? Why is that important to you? How will that have an impact on you?"

These steps create an atmosphere of closeness and trust which encourage young people's willingness to listen to our perceptions. Their willingness to listen is further enhanced when we share our perceptions by using the process of, "I feel _____ about _____ because _____."

PERFECTION IS NOT A REQUIREMENT

To err is human. Mistakes are opportunities to learn. Children are wonderfully resilient and forgiving, especially when we are positive and encouraging much of the time.

My kids will endure many adultisms, "How come you never? Why can't you ever? Surely you realize! How many times do I have to tell you? When will you ever grow up?" when they can count on being treated with dignity and respect in the majority of their dealings with me.

When I *lose it,* they will understand and say, "Dad is having a bad day. Check him out tomorrow."

If they hear the *adultisms* in most of their encounters with me, however, then they will say, "Don't fool with Dad. The odds are that you will encounter a *bad day* any time you go near him. Just get high, get loaded, get away."

We are not suggesting perfection. We are suggesting that we try to bias the outcome so that in most of our encounters we come out ahead.

We can keep working on our own improvement as we work to encourage and motivate others toward improvement. The important thing is to be satisfied with each small step.

Shortly after writing a book on *Developing Capable Young People,* I arrived home. As I drove down my driveway, I perceived my oldest daughter tugging on the mouth of a very expensive horse. What could a father do?

I locked all four wheels, slid to a stop, leaped a five-foot fence, lifted her bodily of the horse and said, "That's it! You will never ride a horse again as long as you live! That I should live to see the day that a descendent of mine should do such a thing to a dumb animal! Don't even touch the horse, I will get it to the barn myself!"

It felt so good.

About an hour later she came to me and said, "Dad, have you calmed down enough yet to talk?"

I rubbed it in, "Well, I really never expected to see anything like that. I was really angry."

She said, "You had every right to be angry. I should not have been riding the horse when I was in that mood."

I said, "Then what is there to discuss?"

She said, "I just wanted to make sure that you meant it when you said I could never ride a horse again as long as I live because you have me signed up for the 'Nationals' this summer, and I wondered if I should make other plans for the summer."

I said, "It was a bit heavy."

She said, "I thought so."

I asked, "Well, what were you expecting?"

She said, "When you were in a more rational frame of mind, we already discussed it. We agreed that if we abused the horse, we would have to give up the privilege of using it for 30 days; or, if it was real serious, for six weeks."

I said, "What were you thinking of?"

She said, "Thirty days."

I said, "I was thinking of six weeks."

She said, "Could it be five?"

When we look at that example, we see a child who had not had my anger projected on her for a long time. She had learned that the worst time to deal with peoples' feelings is when they are in the middle of them.

Her results were directly related to her perceptions, skills, and capabilities. She was motivated by her belief that if she exercised some self-discipline and some judgement and chose her time that she could be potent in affecting and changing what happened to her in life.

SELF-ENCOURAGEMENT

In the art of motivation a lot of attention is given to the superconscious. Those ideas that dominate our thinking when we are not focused on anything else always find expression in our lives somewhere. It has been said, "If you think you are beaten, you are. If you think you can't, you are right."

When moving into a new frontier, we have to image ourselves into the changes that are important. The hard part is getting so many ideas at once that we do nothing.

USE IT OR LOSE IT

An excellent way to insure that we do not lose our enthusiasm and motivation to try the new things we feel inspired to do is to spend a few moments a day in guided meditation and imagery.

The following is a guided meditation which you might like to read into a tape recorder, then get into a comfortable position and allow yourself to experience the results of listening and following the suggestions.

Think back over the chapters you have read and ask yourself:

1. "What is the most important thing I have gotten in touch with or come to realize, or what behavior change do I want to make as a result of reading this book?"

2. Focus on the thought, realization, motivation, or behavior change you would like to make. Reflect for a moment as to why it impresses you as important right now. How can it make a difference in your life and/or the lives of your children? Why did it ring so heavily on your life or your awareness?

3. After you have finished that reflection, imagine yourself actively seeking the opportunity to do something with your new awareness or knowledge. Where is the very first place you intend to apply it? Envision a situation. Envision yourself thinking, doing, feeling, exactly what you want.

4. In your heart, complete the following statement: "As a result of this awareness, the first thing I will do at the first opportunity is _____."

5. Before you go to bed at night, take a leisure moment and recreate that thought process for yourself. Turn that thought over to your superconsciousness and then go off to sleep.

If you follow that guided meditation for three days or more, it will begin to be spontaneous and second nature for you to move in the direction you desire. Close out any significant learning with a clear image of what you can do with it, and it will help you grow and change and learn.

We will improve faster when we avoid the discouragement that occurs whenever we allow ourselves to wallow in thoughts about what we did not accomplish. When we focus our superconscious on the negative, we become locked into negative feelings. If it is important that we help young people focus their superconscious on possibilities, then we must discipline ourselves in that same process. Negative thinking is self-defeating. It focuses on, "What if? If only. I should have. Why didn't I?"

We inoculate ourselves against burnout when we do not allow ourselves to recreate failures or inventory what we didn't accomplish during the day. When we recreate our perceived failures, our superconscious will chatter away throughout the night with messages of inadequacy that will burn out our reserves and destroy the value of our sleep.

No matter what we did or did not accomplish during the day, our last conscious thought before going to sleep should be either an inventory of what we did contribute that we are proud of or a clear vision of what we are going to do tomorrow as a result of the learning of the day.

TAKING THE FIRST STEP

A father who had participated in a ten-day intensive training program in these principles tried this meditation process on the way home, shared that he realized how little time he was investing in his relationship with his young son. He decided he was going to work conscientiously to upgrade that relationship with that little person. He envisioned himself being responsive to his son on a regular basis.

He announced his intentions to his wife. She immediately said, "It will last two days." Not very encouraging.

He replied, "No, this time I think I have a handle on it, and I'll do it."

The next week he was very responsive to his son. His dream was coming true. One day he was reading the evening paper when suddenly he became aware that his son had excitedly tried to communicate something to him, and he had given him only half an ear. His son suddenly wandered off and he only became aware of what had happened as the door closed. He thought, "That is not consistent with my dream."

He put down the paper and went out the door to see what his son wanted. There he was, sitting with his hands on his chin, 'ooking down the street where some boys were playing ball with their dads.

He asked his son, "What was it you wanted?"

His son replied, "Oh, nothing, Dad."

The father persisted, "Now, honey, I sensed your excitement. I just realized I wasn't paying attention to what you were saying. I really want to know."

"Okay, Dad. I'm not big enough to play ball very well, but the other boys down the street are going hiking with their dads. I think I could do that if you would be willing to go with me."

The father said, "Sure, son. I would like that. I'll organize it."

Then a little bell went off in his head because he had been taught that when you treat children as objects or recipients of what you do, you invalidate them. He remembered what he had learned about making children an asset in what you are doing if you want to affirm them. So he said, "Son, let's work together on this. Why don't you talk with your friends? See what kind of places they go hiking so that you can help me organize the trip."

His son immediately went off to get the information from his friends. Later they decided the place they would go. The father avoided the temptation to be directing and said, "Now help me think of the things that we need to take for the trip."

The little boy said, "Something to eat and drink, and a few other things."

They made a list and divided up the responsibilities. They even got some canvas, did some stitching, and made a little knapsack instead of buying one.

The father was delayed a little at work the evening before they planned to leave. When he came home, he found his son asleep on his knapsack by the door so his Dad could not leave him behind.

Dad tucked him into bed and early in the morning carried him out to the car still asleep. Just as the dawn was appearing, the little boy woke up kind of sleepy, looked around, and smiled. He saw the mountains and was quite thrilled. So they stepped out of the car and saw this little peak up the valley. The son said, "Gee, that is fantastic. We could see what the world looks like up there."

They set off up the trail and began discovering the joy of being together in the out-of-doors. Of seeing little minnows in the stream and wading with bare feet when they were hot. It was really early afternoon before they got to the peak.

The father asked, "What did you bring to eat?"

His son answered," Cookies and lemonade."

He had filled the whole pack with cookies and lemonade, which they ate and drank while they enjoyed the beauty that surrounded them. They forgot to watch the time, and suddenly they realized that it was going to be a race to make it back to the car before dark. They took what they thought would be a shortcut.

It was getting dark when they came to a little tumbledown trapper's cabin. There was a wood pile out to the side of the cabin, so they decided not to take a chance on getting lost in the woods. They had enough lemonade and cookies left to make it through the night.

They brought in some firewood and started a little fire in the fireplace. They sat together watching the fire and ate cookies and lemonade. When the fire started to burn down, the father asked the little boy, "Would you go out to the woodpile and get us some more wood before the fire burns down?"

The little boy said, "Sure, Dad."

He jumped up and went around a little corner of the cabin and disappeared. The father sat there looking at the fire until it almost went out, and his son still hadn't come back. He got a little nervous and went to find his son. He went around the little corner in the cabin, and there was the little boy standing at the door of the cabin looking out.

The father asked, "What's the matter, son?"

The little boy said, "It's dark out there, Dad. I can't see the woodpile."

His dad asked, "So how far can you see?"

He said, "Just about one step outside the door, Dad."

The Dad said, "Well, take it Son."

The little boy took one step and his father asked, "Now how far can you see?"

"Just about one more step, Dad."

His father said, "Go ahead and take it."

And step by step the boy made his way to the woodpile. When he turned around, he could see the light in the doorway to come back.

That is how it is for all of us today. The woodpile of our dreams may be a long way off. It can seem dark out there. Most of us will never see the woodpile when it is time to take the first step.

All we will ever be given on this planet is one step at a time. All we'll ever be allowed to see is the first step, and the first step will be different for all of us because our eyes are different heights above the ground. Our confidence is a little different. Our legs are different lengths. No one can take anyone else's first step.

You have learned many possibilities by reading this book. Many of those possibilities may seem far away in the dark.

Choose just one thing you would like to work on. Make it something that seems simple to you. Perhaps you will just eliminate one barrier at a time. Take that first step. You will then see the next step.

Many people spend their whole life standing in the doorway saying, "I'm not going to take any steps until I see the woodpile." They will be there forever.

It is with love and concern that we have shared many steps with you, but we cannot take them for you. All we can do is point a direction and offer encouragement about the wonderful results waiting for you when you reach the woodpile.

If you get lost for a little while, read some more, join a study group, or call a friend for support until you get a perspective on where that woodpile might be so you can begin again — one step at a time.

That is our challenge. Until we have the courage to take the individual next step that we can see, the steps beyond will not be revealed to us because each new step depends upon the one we have just taken.

INOCULATION

The activities presented in the previous chapters serve as an inoculation against the development of characteristics that comprise *high risk* individuals. Most of the concepts and activities presented in this book promote firmness with dignity and respect and teach us to avoid strictness and permissiveness.

The following suggestions and guidelines are based on attitudes which will help parents who want to make changes.

SEEING OUR OWN MISTAKES AS OPPORTUNITIES TO LEARN

One of the authors has written a book on *Positive Discipline*, which stresses the importance of using firmness with dignity and respect when interacting with children. She shares with others that the philosophy of *Positive Discipline* is never humiliating; however, sometimes she behaves in humiliating ways, as illustrated in the following story:

The other day I told my eleven-year-old daughter Mary that she was a spoiled brat.

Mary retorted, "Well, don't tell me later that you are sorry."

I promised, "You don't have to worry, because I'm not."

Mary went to her bedroom, grabbed her copy of *Positive Discipline*, and wrote "phony" on several pages. Five minutes later she came to me, threw her arms around me, and said, "I'm sorry."

I said, "I'm sorry too, honey. I really lost it, didn't I? It is obvious that I was being a spoiled brat when I called you a spoiled brat. I was upset at you for not controlling your behavior, but I didn't control my own behavior. I apologize."

Mary said, "That is okay, Mom, I really was being a brat, and I apologize."

We then talked about a plan for how we would both handle our behavior in the future.

Mary was quick to be the first to apologize because she has experienced many apologies through a process called:

THE THREE R'S OF RECOVERY

1. Recognize (realize mistake)

2. Reconcile (apologize)

3. Resolve (work together on solutions)

Children respond very favorably to this process. They can be feeling very angry and resentful toward an adult who has been disrespectful and humiliating but quick to forgive when an apology is offered. An apology usually creates an atmosphere of support immediately so that positive work on solutions can take place.

The Three R's of Recovery is an excellent model to teach children that mistakes truly are opportunities to learn. Many parents have found that using this process after making a mistake improves the relationship even more than if they had not made a mistake in the first place.

The question has been asked, "Doesn't an apology undermine your authority with children?"

My reply, "I hope so. I am more interested in cooperation, negotiation, and teaching self-discipline than in maintaining my authority."

So often we think of apologizing as *wishy washy* behavior. It can be when a person is self-effacing and apologizes just to please. Apologies are effective when we genuinely recognize that we have behaved in an ineffective manner and want to take steps toward correction.

A few days after the incident with Mary described above, she was talking on the phone with her friend and said, "Oh, Nancy, you are so stupid?" She quickly recovered and said, "I'm sorry, Nancy. If I call you stupid, that means I am being stupid."

Mary had learned to be responsible for her own perceptions and to apologize for being disrespectful.

In an earlier chapter the point was made that we should not apologize for feelings, such as anger, but only for what we might *do* with that anger that is disrespectful to another person.

We also do not need to apologize or feel guilty for doing the best we can with whatever skills and understanding we have. We give young people a good example when we forgive ourselves for our own mistakes and learn from them rather than getting depressed or angry about our mistakes.

HELP CHILDREN SEE MISTAKES AS OPPORTUNITIES TO LEARN

It is not helpful to say, "You are a naughty girl," or even, "You did a naughty thing," but "Whoops, that didn't work. What can we do to fix it?"

We can be open with our own mistakes or areas in which we might be struggling: "I have always struggled with my feelings, and I don't handle that very well. It has cost me a lot at work, and it has cost me a lot in my relationships. Whenever you need to talk about something, I will try, I will do my best."

This attitude encourages children to work at doing something their parents have not mastered. That is very encouraging.

DO NOT EXPECT PERFECTION OF YOURSELF

Sometimes the finest coaches on earth cannot play the game well, but they are terrific at coaching. Every generation has improved over the last generation in many ways, fully showing that human beings can transcend their teachers, their parents, and their environment. How do they do that? When they believe they are capable and can learn and think. They do not believe they are limited by the people they have seen or not seen. They believe they can always imagine a new alternative.

Thousands of parents have been able to help their children accomplish things they themselves couldn't do. A parent who recognizes that he has difficulty exploring his feelings can, at least, learn some ways to help his children be more comfortable with feelings.

Most great discoveries and advancement in the human race

came from people who took the initiative to do something they didn't know how to do and that they had seen no one else do. Successful people aren't limited by what they know how to do right now. They constantly explore new possibilities and put things together in new ways.

CONSISTENCY

Sometimes people make a great issue of consistency, saying, "What can I do when the child's mother, father, or teacher does things differently?" Human beings are beautifully equipped to handle inconsistencies between people and their environment. Children are very good at changing their behavior with each person they deal with depending on what kind of behavior gets the results they are seeking. Having the opportunity to develop different ways of interacting with people can be a very good skill for children to learn.

Once a child develops a capability in one environment (home, school, work, or play) he or she will usually have the flexibility to transfer it to another environment.

PARENTING WITH PERSPECTIVE

The story of Joseph being sold into Egypt could have been judged as a disaster for Jacob. It all depends on your perspective. If he wanted the approval of his neighbors, it was a disaster. They would say, "That man was a prophet and still had a kid sold to the Egyptians by the rest of the family.

But if his long-term goal was to have his children and descendants thrive and survive, then Joseph being sold into Egypt was a great blessing. While his neighbors who didn't approve of Joseph being sold died in the famine, his family moved down and joined Joseph.

It is very important that we don't judge our performance or the things that we do short term.

It is often a mistaken belief to feel "If I was a better parent, I would have better children." Adam and Eve started out walking and talking with God and then had a family. They only batted 50-50 with their first two sons. At least they wrote their experiences down carefully so we could understand what had happened. The basic message they gave is that no matter what you do as a parent, in the end your children will express their individuality. The other message is never to assume that if you deal with two children the same, they will have the same experience. What one son saw as support, the other son saw as rejection and built a case to destroy four lives.

When we have perspective, we can come closer to understanding another person's point of view, or at least understand and respect that we do see things differently. Perspective also usually helps us see the humor in so many things.

SENSE OF HUMOR

Set aside a moment every day to laugh at yourself. If you can't find something genuine to laugh at yourself for, then laugh at yourself for taking yourself too seriously. Laugh at yourself for your humanity. It is much easier to be self-forgiving if you have a sense of humor.

PARENTING ATTITUDES AND PERCEPTIONS

Parenting can be seen as a chore and a burden or as an adventure with unlimited possibilities and opportunities for joy and fulfillment. The difference is merely a matter of attitude and perception.

The purpose of this book is to help parents make changes in attitudes and perceptions that can not only solve everyday problems but help children find success and happiness in any endeavor they choose.

BIBLIOGRAPHY

Adler, Alfred, **What Life Should Mean to You.** New York: G.P. Putnam's Sons, 1958.

Allred, G. Hugh, **How To Strengthen Your Marriage and Family.** Provo, Utah: Brigham Young University Press, 1976.

Allred, G. Hugh, **Mission For Mother: Guiding the Child.** Salt Lake City, Utah: Book Crafts, 1968.

Balswick, J., & Macrides, C. *Parental stimulus for adolescent rebellion.* **Adolescence,** 1975 Summer, Vol. X, No. 38.

Barnes, G. *The development of adolescent drinking behavior. An evaluative review of the impact of the socialization process within the family.* **Adolescence,** 1977, Vol. XII, No. 48. pp. 571-591.

Booz-Allen and Hamilton, Inc., *An assessment of the needs of and resources for children of alcoholic parents.* Prepared for National Institute on Alcohol Abuse and Alcoholism. (Rep. No. PB-241-119; NIAA/NCALI-75/13.) U.S. Nat. Tech. Inform. Serv.; 1974.

Burns, Marilyn. **I Am Not A Short Adult.** Boston and Toronto: Little Brown & Col., 1977.

Calicchia, J.P. *Narcotic addiction and perceived locus of control.* **Journal of Clinical Psychology** 1973, 30, pp.499-504.

Canfield, Jack and Harold Wells. *One Hundred Ways to Enhance Self Concept In the Classroom.* Englewood Cliffs, N.J.: Prentice Hall, 1976.

Clarke-Stewart, K. *Popular primers for parents.* **American Psychologist,** April 1978, pp. 359-369.

Cooker, P. & Cherchia, P. *Effects of communication skill training on high school students' ability to function as peer group facilitators.* **Journal of Counseling Psychology** 1976, **23,** No. 5 pp. 464-467.

Cork, R. Margaret, *The forgotten children.* Alcoholism and Drug Addiction Research Foundation of Ontario; 1969.

Corsini, R.J., & Painter, G. **The Practical Parent.** New York: Harper & Row, 1975.

Dinkmeyer, D., & Dreikurs, R. **Encouraging Children To Learn: The Encouragement Process .** Englewood Cliffs, N.J. : Prentice Hall, 1963.

Dinkmeyer, Don and Gary D. McKay. **Raising a Responsible Child** . New York: Simon and Schuster, 1973.

Dreikurs R. & Soltz, V. **Children: The Challenge** . New York: Hawthorn Books, Inc., 1964.

Dreikurs, R., & Grey, L. A New Approach to Discipline: Logical Consequences. New York: Hawthron Books, Inc., 1968.

Dreikurs, R., Grunwald, B., & Pepper, F. Maintaining Sanity In The Classroom. New York: Harper & Row, Inc., 1971.

Dreikurs, R. Social Equality: The Challenge of Today. Chicago: Contemporary Books, Inc., 1971.

Ducette, J., Wolk, S., & Soucar, E. *A typical pattern in locus of control and nonadaptive behavior.* Journal of Personality 1972, **40**, pp. 287-297.

Duncan, D. *Attitudes toward parents and delinquency in suburban adolescent males.* Adolescence, Vol. XII, No. 50, Summer 1978, pp. 365-369.

Forer, Lucille, The Birth Order. New York, McKay, 1976.

Frankel, J., and Dullaert, J. *Is adolescent rebellion universal?* Adolescence, Summer 1977, Vol. XII, No. 46. pp. 227-236.

Gabel, H. *Effects of parental group discussion on adolescents' perceptions of maternal behavior.* Journal of Community Psychology, Vol. 3 (1), January 1975.

Glenn, H. Stephen. Strengthening The Family , Potomac Press, 1980.

Glenn, H. Stephen & Warner, J. Developing Capable Young People , Hurst, Texas, Humansphere, Inc., 1982.

Gordon, Thomas. P.E.T. — Parent Effectiveness Training . New York: Peter H. Wyden, 1970.

Guzzetta, R. *Acquisition and transfer of empathy by the parents of early adolescents through structured learning training.* Journal of Counseling Psychology 1976, Vol. 23, No. 5 pp. 449-453.

Harmin, Merill, Harold Kirschenbaum, and Sidney Simon. Clarifying Values Through Subject Matter. Minneapolis, MN: Winston Press, 1973.

Herndon, James. How To Survive In Your Native Land. New York: Bantam Books, 1972.

Hetherington, E. *Effects of father absence on personality development in adolescent daughters.* Developmental Psychology 1972, Vol. 7, No. 3.

Hoffman, M. *Fathers absence and conscience development.* Developmental Psychology, 1971, Vol. 4, No. 3.

Jessor, S. & Jessor, R. *Maternal ideology and adolescent problem behavior.* Developmental Psychology 1974, Vol. 10, No. 2, pp. 246-254.

Kandel, D., Kessler, R. and Margulies, R. *Antecedents of adolescent-*

initiation into stages of drug use: A developmental analysis. **Journal of Youth and Adolescence**, Vol. 7, No. 1, 1978, pp. 13-48.

Kvols-Riedler, K. & B. **Redirecting Children's Misbehavior.** Boulder, Colorado: R.D.I.C. Publications, 1979.

Lawson, Gary, Peterson, James, & Lawson, Ann, **Alcoholism And The Family,** Rockville, MD: An Aspen Publication, 1983.

Lesseigne, M. *A study of peer and adult influence on moral benefits of adolescents.* **Adolescence** 1975, Summer, Vol. X, No. 38, pp. 227-230.

Lockwood, A. *The effects of values clarification and moral development criteria,* **Review of Educational Research,** Summer 1978, Vol. 48, No. 3, pp. 325-364.

Lofquist, William, **Understanding The Meaning Of Prevention,** Youth Development Association, Phoenix, AZ, 1980.

Manet, Marsha, **Parents, Peers and Pot,** Vol. I & II, National Institute On Drug Abuse.

Marsella, A. Dubanoski, R., & Mohs, K. *The effects of father presence and absence of maternal attitudes.* **Journal of Genetic Psychology** 1974, **125.**

Nelsen, Jane Ed.D. **Positive Discipline,** Fair Oaks, CA: Sunrise Press, 1981.

Nelsen, Jane Ed.D. **Understanding,** Fair Oaks, CA: Sunrise Press, 1986.

Nihira, K. Usin, A. & Sinay, R. *Perception of parental behavior by adolescents in crisis.* **Psychological Reports** 1975, 37, pp. 787-793.

Norem-Hebeisen, A.A. *Self esteem as a predictor of adolescent drug abuse,* In: **Predicting Adolescent Drug Abuse,** 1975, NIDA.

Nutt, Grady, **Family Time.** 2340 River Road, Des Plaines, Ill 60018: Million Dollar Round Table, 1977.

Plumb, M., D'Amanda, C., & Taintor, Z. *Chemical substance abuse and perceived locus of control.* In: **Predicting Adolescent Drug Abuse,** 1975, NIDA.

Robinson, P. *Parents of beyond control adolescents.* **Adolescence,** Spring 1978, Vol. CIII, No. 49, pp. 109-119.

Robinson, W. *Boredom at school.* **British Journal of Educational Psychology and Psychiatry,** 1975, Vol. 16.

Ryley, Helen, Dinkmeyer, D, Frierson, E., Glenn, S., & Shaw, D., **You've Got To Be Kid-ding.** American Training Center, Boulder, Colorado, 1985.

Scheirer, M. & Kraut, R. *Increasing educational achievement via self-concept change.* **Review of Educational Research,** Winter 1979, Vol. 49, NO 1. pp. 131-150.

Stanley, S. *Family education to enhance the moral atmosphere of the family and the moral development of the adolescents.* **Journal of Counseling Psychology** 1978, Vol. 25, No. 2, pp. 110- 118.

Simon, Sidney. **I Am Lovable and Capable.** Niles, Ill: Argus Communications, 1973.

Small, Jacquelyn. **Becoming Naturally Therapeutic.** Road Runner Road, Austin, TX 78746: Eupsychian Press, 1950.

Stinnett, N. & Taylor, S. *Parent-child relationships and perceptions of alternate life styles.* **The Journal of Genetic Psychology** 1976, 129.

Stone. L. Miranne, A. & Ellis, G. *Parent-peer influence as a predictor of marijuana use.* **Adolescence,** Spring 1979, Vol. XIV, No. 53, pp. 115-122.

Streit, F., *IPAC Evaluation of Open Door Program* and *Evaluation of Project Redirection.* September 1978, Streit Associates, Highland Park, NJ 08904.

Streit, Fred, Halsted, Donald, L. and Pascale, Pietro, J. *Differences among youthful users and nonusers of drugs based on their perceptions of parental behavior.* **The International Journal of Addictions,** Vol. 9, No. 5, pp. 749-755, 1974.

Tuckman, J., & Regan, R. *Ordinal position and behavior problems in children.* **Journal of Health and Social Behavior** 1971, March, 12.

Valles, Jorges M.D., **From Social Drinking to Alcoholism**

Wadsworth, Bary J. **Piaget's Theory of Cognitive Development.** New York and London: Longman, 1971.

Wolk, S., and Brandon, J. *Runaway adolescents' perceptions of parents and self.* **Adolescence** 1977 Summer, Vol. XII, No. 46, pp. 175-187.

SUNRISE PRESS ORDER FORM

To: Sunrise Press   Phone: (916) 961-5551
     9700 Fair Oaks Blvd, Suite C   1-800-456-7770 (orders only please)
     Fair Oaks, CA 95628
Please send the following:

Books:

	Price	Quantity	Amount
RAISING CHILDREN FOR SUCCESS: *Building Blocks for Developing Capable People* by H. Stephen Glenn with Jane Nelsen	$7.95	_____	_____
UNDERSTANDING: Eliminating Stress and Dissatisfaction in Life and Relationships by Jane Nelsen	$ 7.95	_____	_____
POSITIVE DISCIPLINE: Teaching Children Self-Discipline, Responsibility, Cooperation, and Problem-Solving Skills by Jane Nelsen	$ 7.95	_____	_____
COMING HOME: A Collection by Sue Pettit	$ 4.95	_____	_____

Cassette Tapes:

	Price	Quantity	Amount
Developing Capable People (6-Tape Set) by H. Stephen Glenn	$49.00	_____	_____
Involving & Motivating People (Glenn)	$ 8.00	_____	_____
Positive Discipline (Nelsen)	$ 8.00	_____	_____

Posters:

	Price	Quantity	Amount
Positive Discipline Poster set - ten black & white glossy posters (17 x 22)	$10.00	_____	_____

                                       SUBTOTAL _____

California Residents add 6% sales tax
<u>Shipping and handling</u> $1.50 - 1st item _____
   $.50 each additional item **except:** _____
   $2.00 shipping & handling on Poster Set _____
   $2.00 shipping & handling on DCP 6-Tape Set _____
                                     TOTAL _____

METHOD OF PAYMENT (Check One):
_____ Check or Money Order Payable to SUNRISE PRESS enclosed
Charge my _____ MASTERCARD _____ VISA

_____   _____
Charge Card Account Number   Expiration Date

_____
Signature of Authorized Buyer
Ship to _____
Address _____
City _____ State _____ Zip _____

SUNRISE PRESS ORDER FORM

To: Sunrise Press   Phone: (916) 961-5551
      9700 Fair Oaks Blvd, Suite C   1-800-456-7770 (orders only please)
      Fair Oaks, CA 95628
Please send the following:

Books:
	Price	Quantity	Amount
RAISING CHILDREN FOR SUCCESS: *Building Blocks for Developing Capable People* by H. Stephen Glenn with Jane Nelsen	$7.95	_____	_____
UNDERSTANDING: Eliminating Stress *and Dissatisfaction in Life and Relationships* by Jane Nelsen	$ 7.95	_____	_____
POSITIVE DISCIPLINE: Teaching Children *Self-Discipline, Responsibility, Cooperation,* *and Problem-Solving Skills* by Jane Nelsen	$ 7.95	_____	_____
COMING HOME: A Collection by Sue Pettit	$ 4.95	_____	_____

Cassette Tapes:
	Price	Quantity	Amount
Developing Capable People (6-Tape Set) by H. Stephen Glenn	$49.00	_____	_____
Involving & Motivating People (Glenn)	$ 8.00	_____	_____
Positive Discipline (Nelsen)	$ 8.00	_____	_____

Posters:
	Price	Quantity	Amount
Positive Discipline Poster set - ten black & white glossy posters (17 x 22)	$10.00	_____	_____

	SUBTOTAL _____
California Residents add 6% sales tax	_____
<u>Shipping and handling</u> $1.50 - 1st item	_____
$.50 each additional item **except:**	_____
$2.00 shipping & handling on Poster Set	_____
$2.00 shipping & handling on DCP 6-Tape Set	_____
	TOTAL _____

METHOD OF PAYMENT (Check One):
_____ Check or Money Order Payable to SUNRISE PRESS enclosed
Charge my _____ MASTERCARD _____ VISA

_____   _____
Charge Card Account Number   Expiration Date

_____
Signature of Authorized Buyer
Ship to _____
Address _____
City _____ State _____ Zip _____

SUNRISE PRESS ORDER FORM

To: Sunrise Press   Phone: (916) 961-5551
    9700 Fair Oaks Blvd, Suite C   1-800-456-7770 (orders only please)
    Fair Oaks, CA 95628
Please send the following:

Books:

	Price	Quantity	Amount
RAISING CHILDREN FOR SUCCESS: *Building Blocks for Developing Capable People* by H. Stephen Glenn with Jane Nelsen	$7.95	____	____
UNDERSTANDING: Eliminating Stress *and Dissatisfaction in Life and Relationships* by Jane Nelsen	$ 7.95	____	____
POSITIVE DISCIPLINE: Teaching Children *Self-Discipline, Responsibility, Cooperation,* *and Problem-Solving Skills* by Jane Nelsen	$ 7.95	____	____
COMING HOME: A Collection by Sue Pettit	$ 4.95	____	____

Cassette Tapes:

Developing Capable People (6-Tape Set) by H. Stephen Glenn	$49.00	____	____
Involving & Motivating People (Glenn)	$ 8.00	____	____
Positive Discipline (Nelsen)	$ 8.00	____	____

Posters:

Positive Discipline Poster set - ten black & white glossy posters (17 x 22)	$10.00	____	____

                      SUBTOTAL ____

California Residents add 6% sales tax   ____
<u>Shipping and handling</u> $1.50 - 1st item   ____
  $.50 each additional item **except:**   ____
  $2.00 shipping & handling on Poster Set   ____
  $2.00 shipping & handling on DCP 6-Tape Set   ____

                      TOTAL ____

METHOD OF PAYMENT (Check One):
_____ Check or Money Order Payable to SUNRISE PRESS enclosed
Charge my _____ MASTERCARD _____ VISA

_____   _____

Charge Card Account Number   Expiration Date

_____

Signature of Authorized Buyer

Ship to _____

Address _____

City _____ State _____ Zip _____